CRAFTING COZIES

A WRITER'S GUIDE TO BESTSELLING MYSTERIES

INESSA SAGE

CAULDRON PRESS

Crafting Cozies

A Writer's Guide to Bestselling Mysteries

Copyright © 2024 Inessa Sage

Cauldron Press

No part of this book may be reproduced in any form or by any electronic or mechanical means, including information storage and retrieval systems, without permission in writing from the publisher, except by reviewers, who may quote brief passages in a review.

Some characters and events in this book are fictitious. Any similarity to real persons, living or dead, is coincidental and not intended by the author.

All rights reserved.

ISBN 9781989868409 (Paperback Edition)

ISBN 9781989868393 (Electronic Edition)

Cover and interior art by Cauldron Press

www.cauldronpress.ca

© Inessa Sage and www.inessasage.com

Contents

Introduction   v

Chapter 1: What is a Cozy Mystery?   1
Chapter 2: Understanding the Cozy Mystery Reader   5

Part 1: Developing Characters

Creating Compelling Characters   13
Chapter 3: Developing an Amateur Sleuth   17
Sleuth Profile Development Worksheet   31
Chapter 4: Developing the Antagonist   35
Antagonist Profile Development Worksheet   43
Chapter 5: Developing the Supporting Cast   45
Chapter 6: Victim and Suspects   53

Part 2: Creating Settings

Chapter 7: Developing a Cozy Setting   63
Cozy Setting Development Worksheet   71

Part 3: Outline and Plot

Constructing an Engaging Plot   77
Chapter 8: Four-act Structure   81
Chapter 9: The Importance of the Puzzle   91
Chapter 10: Weaving In Subplots   97
Cozy Mystery Beat Sheet   105
Cozy Mystery Beat Breakdown   107

Cozy Mystery Crime Brainstorm	149
Author Murder Board	153

Part 4: Tension and Pacing

Mastering the Art of Pacing	157
Chapter 11: Balancing Action and Introspection	163
Chapter 12: Building Up Suspense	171
Chapter 13: Chapter Structure and Cliffhangers	177

Part 5: Writing Style

Writing Style and Tone	187
Chapter 14: Cozy Mystery Writing Style	191

Part 6: Polishing Your Manuscript

Chapter 15: Revision and Editing Techniques	203
Commonly Overused Words	211

Part 7: Planning a Cozy Series

Chapter 16: Developing a Series	217
Series Bible Template	225
Conclusion	229
About the Author	233

INTRODUCTION

What is it about cozy mysteries that makes them have such a profound hold on their readers?

To answer that, I could go a few different ways. I could begin by telling you all the ways in which mysteries that are cozy at their core draw in a certain type of reader. I could point out that cozy mysteries scratch the itch of clue-solving without the emotional turmoil of a more gritty thriller. I could even talk about the pets because we sure love those in our cozies.

The truth of the matter is, cozy mysteries are simply jolly good fun, aren't they?

No matter where the current market skews, the category of the cozy mystery has been around for quite some time and I do not see it going away anytime soon. In fact, year by year, more readers are welcoming the genre into their TBRs with open arms. To me this says only one thing: cozy mysteries are expanding their reach and they will continue to

Introduction

do so for as long as readers continue to crave a sweeter mystery.

Now, what does that mean for you, dear writer?

That the sky is the limit, of course!

If you're like me and have been reading cozies for a long time, you might be wondering what differentiates this genre from other mysteries and sleuth-based novels. Surprisingly, a lot. My first advice to anyone wanting to get into writing cozies is to read them. A lot. Get sucked into the world of the amateur sleuth and add different types of cozies to your list. The more widely you read in the genre, the more you will develop your own personal style.

Once you are comfortable and want to give writing your very first cozy a try, it's time to pick up this book.

Within these pages, you will discover an entire arsenal developed to help you succeed in the genre. Starting from character development, to setting creation, going into a full plot breakdown of every beat you will use to outline your novel, and a detailed approach to constructing a page-turning whodunit, this book will make sure you have every base covered. We will even discuss such details as pacing, writing style, series development, and editing for cozies.

By the time you're done, you will be an expert in

the cozy mystery and will be well on your way to writing your very own novel.

As a bonus, I am including detailed templates that I use in my own writing to help me with plotting and planning. If you follow along and use the included templates, you will certainly have all you need to write your book. This guide is here to help you in the journey of writing a cozy mystery, so there is no added material that I do not think is necessary for that task. My goal is to get you writing and not to waste your time.

As we move along, if there are terms or tropes that are specific to the cozy mystery genre, I will provide you with the information you need to understand them. When I started writing this book, I made it a point to keep it as evergreen as possible so it can continue to help authors. Because of this, I will refrain from using metrics, stats, and popular examples as those change regularly and I do not want you to get caught up in the hype if it might not be relevant tomorrow. I will, however, include examples from my Orchard Hollow series to show relevance and to stay consistent throughout the book.

Now with that said, I mentioned earlier that my main advice for writers is to read. Can you guess what my second important advice might be?

Introduction

WRITE!

Let's do that, shall we? It is time to get cozy and solve a mystery. Will you join me?

CHAPTER 1

What is a Cozy Mystery?

Before we start writing, there is one pressing question to answer, and that is, you guessed it, what exactly is a cozy mystery?

If you look up the term, you will get a wide variety of definitions which all sound close to the heart of what a cozy is: a mystery that features an amateur sleuth, where violence, sex, and gore happens offstage, and one is set in an intimate community. This sub-genre title was coined in the late 20th century by writers who wanted to recreate the feel of traditional mysteries from the Golden Age of writing. Think Agatha Christie books and you have a pretty good idea of what the Golden Age means.

The emergence of the cozy mystery genre marked a deliberate departure from the darker and grittier themes that had come to dominate mystery fiction. While some authors were drawn to exploring the grittier crimes, others felt a deep affection for the traditional puzzle-solving sleuths and the comforting, quaint settings they inhabited. Thus, the cozy mystery genre was born out of a desire to maintain the essence of classic mystery storytelling while sidling it with warmth, charm, and a sense of community.

There are a few key elements to the cozy that one might not find in other sub-genres of mystery.

The Amateur Sleuth

The first and most important one is the amateur sleuth. More often than not, the protagonist in a cozy mystery stumbles into crime like they're open potholes on the street. While they are reluctant to get involved at first, we quickly discover that they have an intrinsic need to solve mysteries, a need fueled by their character goals. We'll discuss protagonist goals later but for now, it's important to note that the sleuth is usually not a police officer, or at least not an active one, and works on their own terms to solve the crime.

The Setting

The next crucial part of a cozy mystery is the setting. The setting in this genre of writing is almost a character of its own. Contained to a small location (town, specific area of a city, a business), the setting has to be such that clues become easily located. The purpose of this is to give our protagonist a reason to get involved and to get rid of some disbelief in them being able to solve a crime when the police cannot. A good example of using setting for a cozy mystery is the classic game of Clue where the setting is an integral part of gameplay.

The Cast

Much like the setting, the characters that live in the world must be those we want to know more about. And not only because one of them is our villain. The cast surrounding the protagonist is a fun and quirky set of people that each have their own unique personalities. The more well-rounded your side characters are, the more likely the reader will want to follow them through the book and the series. More importantly, it will make the world you're building feel real, something we never want to take lightly.

The Crime

The final ingredient in the cozy mystery is… The mystery itself, of course! Readers of this genre love to solve puzzles and they are right there with your sleuth as they try to navigate details of the crime. Make sure that when you're creating these puzzles that they are difficult but not unsolvable. Everything in a cozy has to lead the reader on a journey and while they might not be able to solve the crime as quickly as your sleuth, they should be able to do it, regardless.

One note on the mystery is it can't be gruesome. All violence needs to stay off the page since the softness of the crimes is what makes cozies so appealing to so many readers.

There are other added details that help the cozy genre stand out, which can be added for an extra flair. Things like animals, crafts, interesting businesses, recipes, humor, and, in the case of my own books, magic, are all elements that shouldn't go ignored. You don't need to include all of them. In fact, please don't unless you're looking to write a tome of a book, but playing on some of these can only build out your world further.

Now that you have a better understanding of the genre, let's move on and talk about the next crucial part of crafting a bestselling cozy: the cozy mystery reader.

CHAPTER 2

Understanding the Cozy Mystery Reader

The cozy mystery reader is an elusive creature with a thirst for truth and a shadow that comes alive after midnight... Just kidding. Sort of. While most readers share the same reading DNA, the cozy mystery reader has a specific set of preferences that make them stand out from the rest. Or at least, make them the perfect candidates to read your future book, dear writer.

In order to write a bestselling whodunit, you must know your target audience inside and out. What do I mean by that?

In the simplest terms, read in the genre.

Make it your mission to read as many cozy mysteries as you can before you start writing your book, as you will probably learn a lot about the craft from that alone. When creating your learning TBR, make sure to include different types of cozies and look for a range of protagonists to get a better idea of how you can structure your story. If I could give you one solid piece of advice, it is simply to read.

But you didn't come to this chapter for that, did you? No, you came here to find out about your audience. Let's do that now!

Reader Profile

Cozy mystery readers are a diverse and eclectic group, spanning a wide range of ages, backgrounds, and lifestyles. While there is no one-size-fits-all description of a cozy mystery reader, they often exhibit certain traits that makes them easier to spot.

Demographically, the age range of cozy mystery readers varies, though it tends to skew more adult. Although I personally know a few friends with teens that also love the genre. Perhaps the rise of the cozy fantasy is giving new light to all things cozy!

Reading Habits and Preferences

Cozy mystery readers have distinct reading habits and preferences that shape their sleuthing. They often enjoy a variety of genres but gravitate towards those that offer a blend of mystery, humor, and character-driven narratives. In addition to cozy mysteries, they may indulge in traditional whodunits, amateur sleuth mysteries, and other sub-genres of crime fiction. Thrillers are a big player in the cozy mystery crowd but because of their generally darker nature, they are not loved by all.

When it comes to book length, cozy mysteries typically fall within the range of 200 to 350 pages, providing readers with a satisfying reading experience that can be enjoyed in a single sitting or over a cozy weekend. In words, you're looking at approximately 55k on the low end and 80k on the higher end of the spectrum. To sum up, write your little heart out!

Most readers of this genre still prefer a paperback over an ebook but we are seeing that change as more books become available in other formats. Audiobooks are starting to take off quite a bit since it allows readers to do other life tasks while also reading. The absolute best of both worlds, if you ask me.

Genre Preferences

As mentioned briefly in the previous chapter, the cozy mystery reader enjoys other elements in their cozies that go beyond the mystery. Shocking, I know!

Some of the more popular things to include are pets, because who doesn't love a puppy sidekick, or a cat that gets into trouble, or even a raccoon as I have in my books. Other than furry, or not furry, companions, tactile crafts are always valued and appreciated. Activities like knitting, baking, and reading are always a hit and will keep your readers interested beyond the main plot of the book.

You should also consider the places where cozy mystery readers spend time and add those into your story. Think bakeries, coffee shops, and book stores. If you can picture a reader curled up with a book there, you have a pretty good location.

To get you started, use this list of elements to spark ideas for your book:

- Pets
- Culinary elements
- Crafts
- Book clubs or reading groups
- Tea parties or coffee gatherings
- Vintage shops or antique stores
- Garden clubs or flower arranging
- Cozy cafes or bakeries
- Farmers markets or local fairs
- Bed and breakfast inns
- Quaint bookstores or libraries
- Historic buildings or landmarks
- Secret societies or clubs
- Ghost stories or legends
- Amateur theater groups or productions

- Bicycles or classic cars
- DIY home renovation projects
- Hidden passages or secret rooms

There are many more elements you can incorporate into your book and I encourage you to keep a notebook nearby at all times. You never know when real life will strike and an idea will form. I often pull from my life and daily activities to round out my stories.

Other things to consider

The most important thing to keep in mind about cozy mystery readers is they are starved for knowledge. The reason they heavily gravitate toward the genre is not only because it gives them a chance to test their puzzle-solving skills, but it also introduces them to worlds they may not find in other styles of fiction. Because of this, many cozies will give the reader information on places and cultures that might be otherwise prove out of reach to them. Perhaps you can stage your mystery in a castle in Ireland, or allow the reader a glimpse into the world of competitive chess, or even take them on a trip to an underground vineyard. Whatever your story includes, write it like a movie and give these readers the full immersive experience. They should come out of reading your book as experts in the field.

While readers of the genre will continue to morph and change, and we hope they do so we can get even more people reading cozies, the core of the reader remains the same. Try to cater to your reader's intrinsic needs when you are writing your story and you will always find someone who loves your book.

Speaking of the core of cozies, I think it's high time we talk about the center of the cozy mystery: the characters. Meet me in the next chapter to get to know the people who will make your whodunit a story to remember.

PART 1
DEVELOPING CHARACTERS

CREATING COMPELLING CHARTACTERS

The heart of every book, and the main reason readers fall in love with stories, lies in the characters that live in that world. The people that will become our best friends, our most despised villains, and our trusty sidekicks that never fail to make us laugh. In a cozy mystery, it is that much more imperative to create compelling characters since they will be the driving force behind the mystery. Going back to my earlier example of the classic board game Clue, there would be no murder if the butler didn't pick up a candlestick. More so, there would be no story there if we didn't have a detective on the job.

Every character in your cozy should have a purpose. Whether they are solving the crime, committing it, or are simply around for comical relief, the characters you write should be memorable. That is to say, a reader should be able to pick them out of a lineup… See what I did there? Haha!

There are many ways in which you can approach the development of compelling and rounded characters. The following are a few rules of thumb to follow and we will go into further detail on all of them in the upcoming chapters.

1. Know Your Setting:

Cozy mysteries often take place in small, close-knit communities where everyone knows everyone else's business. Your characters should reflect the quirks and idiosyncrasies of your chosen setting. Consider how their personalities are shaped by their surroundings, whether it's a small English village or a bustling coastal town. Use vivid descriptions and subtle details to bring the setting to life through your characters.

2. Give Them Flaws and Quirks:

Perfect characters are forgettable characters. To make your protagonists and supporting cast memorable, give them flaws, quirks, and imperfections. Maybe your amateur sleuth is a gardener with a tendency to let her curiosity get the better of her. Perhaps the local baker has a penchant for gossip but a heart of gold. These flaws and quirks not only make your characters more relatable, but also provide opportunities for growth and development throughout the story.

3. Create Compelling Backstories:

Every character has a story, and it's often their experiences that shape who they are in the present.

Take the time to develop rich backstories for your characters, including their upbringing, past relationships, and significant life events. These backstories not only add depth to your characters but also provide potential motives and secrets that can drive the plot forward.

4. Focus on Relationships:

One of the joys of cozy mysteries is the relationships that connect the characters. Whether it's the bond between siblings, the rivalry between neighbors, or the budding romance between two unlikely partners, relationships drive the drama and intrigue of the story. Spend time developing these relationships, exploring the dynamics between characters, and how they evolve over the course of the mystery.

5. Balance Humor and Heart:

Cozy mysteries often blend humor with heartwarming moments, creating a delightful reading experience. Infuse your characters with a sense of humor, whether it's through witty dialog, slapstick antics, or dry sarcasm. But don't forget to show their more vulnerable side, allowing readers to empathize with their struggles and root for their triumphs.

6. Leave Room for Growth:

The best characters are the ones who grow and change over the course of the story. Give your characters room to evolve, facing challenges and overcoming obstacles that force them to confront their flaws and become better versions of themselves. Whether it's the amateur sleuth solving her first case or the grumpy neighbor learning to let down his guard, character growth adds depth and complexity to your cozy mystery.

As I always say, nothing is set in stone when it comes to writing, but developing characters that your readers want to see on the page is hard to argue with. While there are many characters that form the cozy community, there is one that stands above the rest. Can you guess which one?

That's right! Your amateur sleuth. Let's see how we can write a detective that not only solves the crime but steals your readers' hearts in the process.

CHAPTER 3

Developing an Amateur Sleuth

Now that you have had a chance to think about the characters in your cozy mystery, it's time to build the detective next door. The cozy mystery sleuth is an elusive creature that depends on sharpened intellect and deductive skills to solve crimes that stump even the police. If that sounds like a far stretch from reality, that's the point! We want to entertain our readers and give them sleuths to root for throughout the tremulous journey of uncovering clues and getting the puzzle put together.

After all, what would a cozy mystery be without a sleuth who didn't butt their nose in where it didn't belong?

When you're building your amateur sleuth, there are several factors to consider. One of the main things to keep in mind is that they have to be relatable and likeable. Unlike other genres, cozy mystery readers do not crave an unreliable narrator, as they want to feel like the sleuth you have put on the page can be someone they might know in real life; perhaps even be them. To do so, we must create a sleuth that is average but with above average skills.

Does that sound contradictory? Good! We want our sleuth to surprise people. With that in mind, let's begin sketching out the amateur sleuth anatomy.

Profile

Begin by fleshing out the basic profile of your sleuth. Are they young or old, introverted or outgoing, analytical or intuitive? Consider their background, upbringing, and social circles. Perhaps they're a retired teacher with a knack for crossword puzzles or a freelance writer with a keen eye for detail.

When creating a profile for your sleuth, I find it helpful to cast them first. Think of yourself as a movie director who is auditioning actors for a role. Hop online and search the depths of the internet for images of people that remind you of your sleuth. Please remember that this is for your own private use and for this exercise only. We cannot use online images for any commercial use without the proper licensing. That includes social media promotion of your book.

Once you have your sleuth in the front of your mind, pull out a notebook or your preferred writing program and note their appearance. You want to be as detailed as possible when getting to know your sleuth. By the end of this exercise, they should feel like a long-time friend and not a fictional character. There are many online questionnaires you can fill out, and I offer character profile sheets in my YouTube community, as well as many other plotting resources.

When I was working on A Grave Roast, the first book in my paranormal cozy mystery series, developing Piper was one of the more fun activities prior to beginning to write. I worked out her physical appearance, drew a map of her home, found pictures of cafes that resembled what would later become Bean Me Up, and even made a sample playlist she might listen to. By the end, I had a fully developed sleuth that could walk amongst us mere humans.

Flaws

Imperfections are the brushstrokes that give depth to your protagonist. Maybe your sleuth is overly curious, often jumping to conclusions without all the facts. Or perhaps they have a tendency to mistrust others, stemming from a past betrayal. These flaws not only humanize your character, but also provide avenues for growth throughout the story.

Since there are no perfect people, there can be no perfect characters. Your sleuth is no exception to the rule. When thinking of your sleuth, try to inject as many real life flaws as you can without going over the top. I find two or three flaws cast a good balance without making the sleuth come across as a walking disaster.

Often, the sleuth's history and backstory will play into their flaws, so try to get a good idea of what your character has been through before the starting point of the novel. Were they fired from a job and had to start over? Did they get broken up with by someone they thought was their forever after? Have they always been a bit of a loner with trouble making friends? The more history your sleuth has, the better. But do remember that this part is mostly for your own purposes. The reader is there for the crime and not a history lesson, so if you are going to be discussing your sleuth's past, do it in small batches throughout the novel. Or not at all.

Going back to Piper, when thinking of her flaws, I added ones that were both physical and emotional to paint her in a more realistic light. After deciding on a past of failed relationships, money troubles, and an absent mother, I had my sleuth. She's clumsy to a fault, doesn't make friends easy, but has determination up the wazoo after years of having to take care of herself.

Occupation

The sleuth's occupation can serve as both a window into their world and a source of expertise. A librarian might possess a wealth of knowledge about obscure topics, while a chef could use their culinary skills to uncover clues. The key is to integrate their profession seamlessly into their sleuthing endeavors, allowing it to both aid and challenge them along the way. As a rule of thumb, try to stick to professions that are not solitary to give your sleuth the opportunity to run into people often.

The place where your protagonist will work will also serve as a side character. For example, a sleuth that owns a bakery gives you the chance to tap into culinary cozies and share recipes with your readers as you write.

The Arc

The emotional development of the amateur sleuth is one of my most cherished activities when I am planning a book. Not only does thinking about your protagonist's arc help you visualize their progression through the story, but it can also spark ideas for plot points. You can use those in later chapters of this book when we discuss story outlines. More so, though, a sleuth with an arc that fits the genre will add to your protagonist's qualities and help the reader connect with them better. If you're unsure of what an arc is, a character arc is the trajectory of change a character undergoes throughout a story, from their initial state to a transformed version of themselves.

There are many types of character arcs you can sample from and use in order to design the way your sleuth moves through the plot. Some of the most widely used arcs are:

1. The Hero's Journey:

Originating from myth and folklore, the Hero's Journey is perhaps the most well-known character arc. It follows the protagonist as they venture into the unknown, face trials, and challenges, and ultimately emerge victorious, transformed by their experiences. This arc is characterized by stages such as the Call to Adventure, the Road of Trials, and the Return with the Elixir.

2. The Redemption Arc:

Redemption arcs center around characters who have fallen from grace, either through their own actions or external circumstances. Throughout the story, they seek forgiveness and redemption, striving to atone for their past mistakes. This arc is often marked by moments of remorse, self-reflection, and acts of selflessness.

3. The Transformation Arc:

Transformation arcs focus on characters who undergo radical changes in their beliefs, values, or worldview. Whether it's a shift from cynicism to hope or ignorance to enlightenment, these characters experience profound inner growth that reshapes their identity. Transformation arcs often involve moments of epiphany, self-discovery, and acceptance.

4. The Anti-Hero Arc:

Anti-hero arcs feature protagonists who lack conventional heroic qualities but are nonetheless compelling and complex. These characters move with moral ambiguity, often operating in shades of gray rather than black and white. Anti-heroes may struggle with their darker impulses or confront societal norms, challenging readers to reconsider traditional notions of heroism.

While you can pick any arc to guide your sleuth, I have found that a combination of the hero's journey and the transformation arcs are a good guide for a cozy mystery. It gives our sleuths just enough ups and downs to learn valuable lessons while staying on track with solving the mystery.

For those who are visual learners, I am including a sketch of a sample arc so you can picture what it would look like on paper. Once you start making notes about your amateur sleuth, see if you can slot the corresponding arc points on this graph to make sure they fit the correct positions. When studying the graph, note that the sleuth starts on neutral ground, rises in emotional development, hits a slight low in the middle of the book and begins to build themselves back up from there. In the last act, your sleuth should be leveling out their arc and slowly getting back to a neutral state.

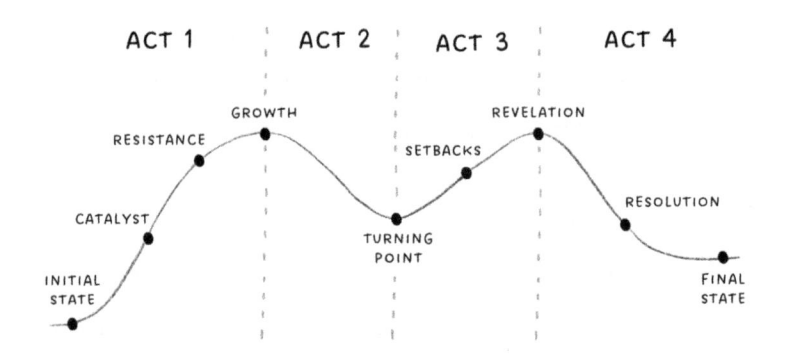

```
    ACT 1    |    ACT 2    |    ACT 3    |    ACT 4
             |             |             |
             |   GROWTH    |  REVELATION |
    RESISTANCE   ●         |      ●      |
        ●    |    \  SETBACKS  /    |
           /   |      \   ●   /     |    RESOLUTION
   CATALYST/  |       \ /     |         ●
        ●    |     TURNING    |          \
  INITIAL    |      POINT     |           ●
   STATE     |                |         FINAL
     ●       |                |         STATE
```

Motivation

What drives your amateur sleuth to solve mysteries? Is it a thirst for justice, a desire to protect their community, or simply a love of puzzles? Understanding their underlying motivations will inform their actions and decisions throughout the story, lending authenticity to their character arc.

More often than not, your sleuth will become involved in the crime out of sheer necessity. Whether they are being framed for it or they are in a position of specific knowledge, they cannot walk away. Look deep into your protagonist's heart and figure out why they need to get involved. If you find the motivation is lackluster, raise the stakes. Give them doorways they have to go through.

When I was first outlining A Grave Roast, Piper's motivations were unclear. Because she is a witch, there were many directions I could have taken. To put her in a position of being unable to refuse the call of the mystery, I dumped the first body in her place of business and made her a prime suspect. Combine that with some magic and bam! We have ourselves a motive.

Goals

Set tangible goals for your sleuth to pursue throughout the narrative. Perhaps they're determined to prove their worth in a male-dominated field or to mend fractured relationships strained by their obsession with solving mysteries. These goals add layers to your protagonist's journey, driving the plot forward while deepening their personal stakes.

Your sleuth's goals should be two-fold: external and internal. While the two sometimes intercept, they are more often very different from one another, allowing you to push and pull your character as they make decisions in the case. When thinking of the types of goals you are assigning to your protagonist, consider both types.

An external goal is one that is one that can be achieved with material rewards. In the case of Piper, her external goal was to stay out of debt by reopening the cafe—the one that closed down on account of a dead body.

Internal goals have to do with anything that cannot be seen by the naked eyes. Your sleuth's personal growth will often be affected by their internal goals. Piper's internal goal was to figure out her malfunctioning magic, so she didn't feel like a disappointing low point in her powerful paranormal family history. This internal goal drove the story by giving Piper opportunities to work on her magic skills throughout the investigation.

Internal Conflict

Beneath the surface of your amateur sleuth's exterior lies a messy web of internal conflict. Perhaps they grapple with self-doubt, haunted by past failures that threaten to overshadow their present investigations. Alternatively, they might struggle with ethical dilemmas, torn between upholding the law and bending the rules to achieve justice. By exploring these inner conflicts, you not only add depth to your sleuth's character, but also create compelling avenues for growth and self-discovery.

When you combine your sleuth's flaws, their internal goals, and motivations for solving the crime, you are putting a lot on their shoulders. Any one of us would probably run for the hills if we encountered as many dead bodies as our sleuths do. But let's hold the disbelief at bay for now. This is a cozy mystery after all!

Instead of hiding away, the amateur sleuth rises to the occasion and, by doing so, they throw themselves into having to deal with their own internal conflicts. They may want to solve the crime, but their past suggests that they haven't been able to lead on decisions before. Whatever your sleuth's inner conflict, they must work through them as they take on the antagonist and come out on top.

Or at least avoid therapy...

Romance Subplot

Introduce a romantic subplot to add an extra layer of intrigue to your sleuth's journey. This could take the form of a budding relationship with a fellow investigator, a rekindled flame from their past, or even a love triangle that complicates their sleuthing efforts. The key is to weave this romantic thread organically into the narrative, allowing it to both complement and intersect with the central mystery, while also providing moments of vulnerability and emotional depth for your protagonist.

Keep in mind that the romance is to be clean and all spicy scenes are to be kept off the page or in your head only. The attention must always be on the mystery.

To add to that, if you do have a triangle, it must be resolved before the end of the book, or a few books in if you are writing a series. Dragging on a romantic subplot is a sure way to aggravate your readers. If you are writing a longer series, consider using multiple subplots as you write each book, so there is a chance for added layers without overkill (pun intended).

Other Subplots

Beyond romance, consider incorporating additional subplots that intersect with your sleuth's central investigation. Perhaps they become embroiled in a community feud that sheds light on the motives of potential suspects, or they uncover long-buried secrets that threaten to upend the lives of those around them. These subplots not only serve to deepen the mystery at hand but also provide opportunities for your sleuth to showcase their resilience, resourcefulness, and compassion in the face of adversity.

In Orchard Hollow, we have a romance subplot with a vampire in the first and second book, which helped me add all the feels and inject a touch of humor. However, the main subplot that carries throughout the series is a secondary mystery as we watch Piper slowly discover why her mom left and what is really happening to her odd magic. By adding another mystery to the background of the series, I was able to make readers go from book to book, waiting to solve it.

Quirks and Habits

Finally, sprinkle in some quirks and habits to make your sleuth memorable. Maybe they have a penchant for collecting vintage teacups or a habit of jotting down observations in a worn-out notebook. These small details not only add charm to your character but also serve as potential clues or plot devices in future mysteries.

In the next section, I included a sleuth profile development template that you can use to start brainstorming your very own protagonist. I recommend taking your time with this as, depending on the length of your book and series, you will have to live with your main character for some time. After you're happy with your amateur sleuth, it will be time to put some obstacles in their way. One main obstacle is another character that is incredibly fun to design. Can you guess who this might be?

If your answer was the antagonist, then you are correct! Let's give our sleuth someone to be afraid of in the upcoming chapter.

SLEUTH PROFILE DEVELOPMENT

Your sleuth's profile

- Name:
- Age:
- Occupation:
- Physical Description:
- Backstory:
- Motivation for Sleuthing:
- Quirks/Habits:
- Strengths:
- Weaknesses:
- Relationships (Family, Friends, Romantic Interest):

Your Sleuth's Character ARC

1. Initial State:

Describe your character at the beginning of the novel. What are their defining traits, flaws, and motivations? How do they feel about their life and the world around them?

2. Catalyst:

What inciting incident or mystery propels your character into action? How does this event disrupt their ordinary life and force them to confront new challenges?

3. Resistance:

How does your character initially react to the mystery or conflict? What obstacles or doubts prevent them from fully embracing their role as a sleuth? What fears or insecurities hold them back?

4. Growth:

Describe the key moments or experiences that push your character out of their comfort zone and compel them to change. How do they overcome obstacles and learn from their mistakes? What skills or insights do they gain along the way?

5. Turning Point:

Identify the pivotal moment in your character's arc where they fully commit to solving the mystery and pursuing justice. What motivates this shift in attitude or behavior? How does it impact their relationships and interactions with other characters?

6. Setbacks:

What setbacks does your character encounter on their journey? How do these challenges test their resolve and force them to reassess their approach to solving the mystery? How do they bounce back from failure?

7. Revelation:

What discoveries or revelations does your character make over the course of the investigation? How do these revelations reshape their understanding of the mystery and their place in the world? What new perspectives or truths do they uncover?

8. Resolution:

Describe how your character's arc culminates in the resolution of the mystery. How have they changed or grown since the beginning of the novel? What lessons have they learned, and how do they apply them to their future actions?

9. Final State:

Reflect on your character's journey and describe who they have become by the end of the novel. How have their experiences shaped their personality, values, and relationships? What lingering questions or challenges remain for them to address in future adventures?

CHAPTER 4

Developing the Antagonist

What would a cozy mystery be without a villain? More so, what would your protagonist be without an antagonist getting in their way?

Both are very good questions and ones we will answer as we work to develop an antagonist that is three-dimensional and has believable motives. As you may have guessed, the motive for the big bad in your book is key to creating an antagonist readers love to hate. Cozy mystery readers adore knowing that the crimes on the page are happening for a reason. This is not the genre for the typical Bond villain who is only evil for the sake of being evil. We want our readers to feel that in the right circumstances, they could have also toed the line between good and bad.

When you are starting to work on your antagonist, always start with a motive. But there are several other factors to consider when crafting your villain. Let's take a look at the parts that make up the antagonist in detail.

Motive: Discover the Why

Every antagonist needs a compelling reason for their actions, something that drives them to commit the crime at the heart of the mystery. Motives in cozy mysteries often revolve around personal gain, revenge, jealousy, or even protecting a dark secret. Consider the antagonist's backstory, relationships, and personal struggles to develop a motive that feels authentic and drives their actions.

The motive should always take the victim into consideration. You want to ask yourself the following questions when coming up with a motive:

- How is the victim in the way of the antagonist getting what they want?
- Can the antagonist get their way without resorting to heinous crimes?
- Why is this the time for them to strike?

Means: The Tools of Deception

Once you've established the motive, consider how your antagonist will execute their plan. What resources do they have at their disposal? Are they cunning enough to manipulate others into carrying out their bidding, or do they prefer a more hands-on approach? The means by which the antagonist carries out their crime should align with their personality, skills, and resources, adding depth to their character and making their actions believable.

When I was developing the antagonist in Cafe au Slay, I needed them to blend in with others because the crime was narrowed to the small community of customers in Piper's Cafe. In order to accomplish this, I made the villain someone no one would suspect. In fact, it was someone most would root for. On the surface, they were kind and clever, but beneath was a brilliant mind that planned the crime for years. I made sure that the antagonist had access to the victim and the means to frame others for their crime.

Alibi: Planting a False Trail

A thought out alibi can make or break an antagonist's plan. When you're plotting your villain's alibi, think about how it will deflect suspicion away from them, since that would be the main goal. This might involve adding a false timeline, manipulating witnesses, or even committing a secondary crime to throw off investigators (a favorite amongst cozy mystery readers.) Crafting a convincing alibi adds an extra layer of challenge for your sleuth and keeps readers guessing until the truth is revealed.

One thing you want to incorporate into your alibi is a loop hole. Something that your sleuth will have trouble seeing right away but will figure out in the end and solve the case. The breaking apart of the alibi can add a secondary element to solving the puzzle or act as the "Aha!" moment when your sleuth finally puts the pieces together.

Plan to Get Away: Escaping Justice

Antagonists in cozy mysteries are often masterminds who carefully plan their escape route in advance. Consider the steps your antagonist will take to evade capture and disappear into the shadows. This might involve fleeing the scene of the crime, lying low in a remote location, or even assuming a new identity. By developing a detailed escape plan, you can raise the stakes for your protagonist and create tension as they race against the clock to catch the culprit before they slip away.

One note of advice when formulating an escape plan is to try to make it as relevant to your antagonist as possible. In other words, don't make your villain plan to escape on a private jet when they're out of work. Private jets are expensive…

It also helps to plan clues to the escape plan ahead of time. In Six Brews Under, for example, the villains were planning to frame another person for two murders. By slowly trickling in negative traits for the scape goat, I was able to keep the reader guessing and throw them off track until the very end.

Clues: Dropping Bread Crumbs

Even the most clever antagonist is bound to leave behind clues that can lead to their downfall. Consider the ways in which your villain might inadvertently leave traces of their involvement in the crime, whether it's a misplaced item, a slip of the tongue, or a subtle change in behavior. These clues should be strategically placed throughout the story, leading your protagonist and readers closer to uncovering the truth behind the mystery.

While you can add clues as you plot and as you write, I find the best way to make sure you are leading the reader on a wild goose chase is to do so after your draft is complete. What I usually do is have an open document while I write that I label "Editing Notes." In this document, I add clues as they come to me while drafting to be incorporated later on. Then, when I am finished with the first draft, I backtrack and add these hints into the story.

When positioning the clues, try to think with all of your senses. Since clues are not always physical, it is important to add depth to how your sleuth solves the crime. Think of smells that might trigger a realization later, a sound they may have heard that seems familiar, the way a fabric might feel in their fingers. Use everything in your arsenal to round out the clues in the story. If you're writing an animal cozy, don't forget to employ those adorable pets. Dogs can help sniff out clues, cats can dig them up, even cute little hamsters can put their paws to good use.

At the end of the book, we want the readers to flip through the pages to see what they may have missed. More so, we want them to become detectives themselves as they come along for the ride with your amateur sleuth.

Character Development: Humanizing the Villain

Lastly, don't forget to flesh out your antagonist's character beyond their role as the villain. Give them depth, complexity, and a hint of humanity that makes readers question their motives and actions. Explore their backstory, inner conflicts, and moral dilemmas to create a well-rounded antagonist.

Going back to the Bond villain and their evil laugh and fluffy white cat. While that villain has a time and a place, in cozy mysteries, readers are expecting a more personal antagonist. Try to design your villain the same way you would your sleuth, in extreme detail. If you find yourself loathing the fictional character you created, you've done your job well.

But sleuths and antagonists are not the only people in a cozy mystery, are they? What would our story be without the supporting cast? A pretty short and boring adventure, I'd say. In the next chapter, we're going to go over how you can use the other people integral to the mystery to drive the plot forward.

ANTAGONIST PROFILE DEVELOPMENT

Antagonist's Profile

- Name:
- Background:
- Motivation:
- Personality Traits:
- Secrets:

Other Notable Details

1. Alibi:

Initial Alibi: Where were they when the crime occurred?

Alibi Development: How is the alibi investigated and potentially disproven?

2. Relationships:

Victim: Connection between the victim and the antagonist.

Sleuth: Connection between the sleuth and the antagonist.

3. Method:

How: How was the crime committed?

Weapon/Tool: What was used to commit the crime?

Disposal: How did the antagonist attempt to cover their tracks?

4. Motive:

Primary Motive: The main reason behind the crime.

Secondary Motives: Any additional reasons or factors that influenced the crime.

5. Character Development:

Evolution: How does the antagonist's character evolve throughout the story?

Doubts and Fears: Internal conflicts or fears they may experience as suspicion mounts.

6. Character Depth:

Backstory: Any relevant backstory that adds depth to the antagonist's character.

Internal Conflicts: Conflicts or dilemmas the antagonist faces throughout the story.

CHAPTER 5

Developing the Supporting Cast

A good rule of thumb for designing the characters that live in the same vicinity as your sleuth is to make them as different from one another as you can. There will be passerby characters that fade into the background and they are essential to show that our sleuth does not live in a vacuum, but they are not what this chapter is about. In this section, we are talking about the cast that gets page time.

A cozy mystery is nothing without the fun, unique community that it takes place in. If you recall, the feeling of community is what sets this genre apart from other mysteries and is integral to reader's expectations being met. In order to form a realistic community, there are several factors to consider when developing the side characters.

When you are beginning to plot your novel, have a page (or two or three) dedicated to the cast of your mystery. On it, make notes about specific personality traits, ticks, common phrases, and other elements that help identify people. Then when you are thinking of characters to add to your cast, pull from these so everyone has a special way about them that isn't repeated in other characters in your book. The more unique elements that you can give to your characters, the more the readers will remember them down the line.

Are you ready, dear writer? It's time to start thinking about the people that make up your world!

Town Dynamics and Community Spirit

In a cozy town setting, the supporting cast is often made of a close-knit community with interconnected lives and histories. Think about how your sleuth fits into the preexisting relationships in your setting. Are they a native resident or a newcomer? How do they deal with and react to small-town life?

Depending on your sleuth's position in the society they occupy, they might have doors open or close for them. Try to imagine your sleuth's everyday life and the people they might interact with. If they own a business, who are their customers? Who are the other business owners on the street?

These are the people your sleuth will have the most in common with and the ones that will become repeated characters in the book or series. The most important thing to keep in mind is that the community has to give off the sense that they band together. Common themes in cozy mystery communities are gossip and found family, both of which can be used to further your plot and add humor.

Local Flavor and Quirks

From the nosy neighbor who knows everyone's business to the quirky shop owner obsessed with ceramic garden gnomes, these characters add color and charm to the narrative. Use their interactions with your sleuth to show the town's personality and atmosphere.

We all have those few people that we will forever remember, and your fictional town should evoke the same emotion. Try to envision the people in it as best as possible. If you're having trouble building out a well-rounded cast that all have unique personalities, taking cues from real life is a great way to stay on top of it. I usually have a small notebook on me where I take notes of funny things that happen in real life, comments people make that I want to remember, and general ideas I think of as I'm spending days outside.

In one of the Orchard Hollow books, Piper and

Joe had an epically disastrous date that involved bumped heads, hot sauce in eyes, and a whole lot of banter. Sadly, that instance came from my own life experience and a hilarious dinner I had with my husband. Use what you know! You will write it best.

Find yourself stuck and searching for character traits? Pack it up and go outside. Taking walks is a surprisingly easy and wonderful way to get out of a slump and develop fresh ideas. You'd be surprised how many of your characters you can develop after a simple walk or visit to a local cafe.

Family Ties and Friendships

Don't forget about your sleuth's connections to their family members, friends, and neighbors. These relationships can provide crucial support, comic relief, or unexpected complications as the mystery unfolds.

In Orchard Hollow, I gave Piper a difficult family history. Hashtag mommy issues was my sleuth's base way of existing for the first three books of the series. Her grandmother, who raised her, passed away, leaving Piper to figure life out on her own. With an absent mother—who is part of a bigger mystery across the books—my sleuth was left entirely alone. This was done with purpose. I specifically made Piper lonely so I could introduce people into her life and show her character arc unfold through the plot of the books. It also gave me a chance to show Piper's character traits in her interactions with new people.

Local Institutions and Traditions

Incorporate local institutions and traditions into the fabric of your cozy town, from the bustling town square to the annual bake-off or harvest festival. These elements provide opportunities for the protagonist to interact with a diverse range of characters and to uncover clues hidden amidst the town's traditions.

Secrets and Intrigues

Every cozy town has its secrets, and the supporting cast is often privy to a wealth of gossip, rumors, and hidden agendas. Use the supporting cast to hint at buried secrets and unresolved conflicts that may hold the key to solving the mystery.

Another good way to use the community's secrets is in the overarching mystery in a series or secondary plots. We will discuss both in more detail later in the book, but for this section, I'd like to note that community secrets can often extend beyond the main mystery. You can create characters whose entire purpose is to be secretive or closed off. This will make them more believable, as many readers would have encountered similar personalities in real life.

Evolution of Relationships

Pay attention to the evolution of relationships throughout the story. As the mystery unfolds, characters may grow closer or drift apart, alliances may shift, and long-held grudges may come to light. Allow these developments to shape the narrative organically, deepening the emotional stakes for both the sleuth and the cast. The longer the series of books you are writing, the more the characters will grow and evolve. Since relationships often change with time, don't be afraid to do the same with the cast in your books.

Perhaps the next-door neighbor gets into a new relationship with someone the sleuth doesn't like. Or maybe the rival bakery owner will later become our sleuth's partner in crime or best friend. Dig deep into these relationships as you write and see how you can change them into new perspectives.

Sense of Belonging and Home

Ultimately, the relationships between the protagonist and the supporting cast should evoke a sense of familiarity and friendship. Whether it's sharing a meal at the local diner, attending a community event, or simply exchanging pleasantries on the street, these moments of connection reinforce the cozy atmosphere of the setting and the bonds that tie the town together.

In my books, Piper Addison has spent all of her life in Orchard Hollow and, with such, she knows the people there inside and out. I used nicknames and slang when having people interact with her to show how comfortable the sleuth feels in the town. I also incorporated moments of reflection from Piper's perspective when she describes the surrounding characters that show the reader her connections in town.

Lastly, as we did with our sleuth, it helps to keep a visual reminder of the people in your cozy mystery. I find that having pictures of the characters in my worlds allows me to tap into their voice better when writing since I can imagine how they would behave based on their physical appearance. It also helps me add details like smells, sounds, fashion sense, jewelry, and other small elements that make for well-rounded characters.

Whoever you choose to add to your mystery, take your time with them. The more you spend on each character, the more they will come to life. You also want to keep that in mind when your sleuth encounters these people for the first time on the page; descriptions can go a long way in a cozy mystery and can help instantly set the mood for your readers.

CHAPTER 6

Victim and Suspects

The final stop on our tour of all things character building will be in the land of victims and suspects. Since we wouldn't have a cozy mystery without someone in the center of the crime and a group of people who could have done it, we need to take some time to design the characters that play such an important part in the plot.

This is where we go back to the classic murder mystery and the ways in which the sleuth navigates through the spiderweb of suspects until the killer is found. More often than not, your sleuth will have at least three suspects to interview and more might be added as they uncover new clues. The purpose of having a solid lineup of suspects is to not only confuse the reader and throw them off track, but to give the puzzle the depth it needs.

We will discuss the suspects and how to position them shortly, but for now, I'd like to start with the character that triggers the investigation: the unsuspecting victim of the crime.

Victim: Catalyst for the mystery

The character that you will use to throw your sleuth into the story has to fit certain criteria. Cozy mystery readers have come to expect the crime to happen, or in many instances, the body to drop fairly early on, which means your victim needs to appear in the story in the first few chapters.

When developing the victim, there are a couple of things to keep in mind.

Whether it's a kindly old librarian or a misunderstood artist, imbue your victim with qualities that resonate with your audience. Provide glimpses into their life and form a connection between readers and the character. Remember, the more invested readers are in the victim, the more they'll root for the amateur sleuth to uncover the truth.

Alternatively, you can give the victim negative qualities and make them the type of person anyone might have wanted to get rid of. Going in this direction, you can expand your suspects to a longer list and really give your sleuth a run for their money. And the reader alongside with them. Do keep in mind not to drag out the investigations as too much sleuthing and not enough action can slow down the pace.

Resist the temptation to create a one-dimensional victim. Complexity adds richness to the narrative, keeping readers engaged as we get closer to the heinous act to come.

In A Grave Roast, the first victim entered Piper's life in the first chapter. We got to know him better, felt a connection to him through the banter he had with Piper, and even rooted for the two to become fast friends. There was a history between the victim and the sleuth that I positioned very early on to give Piper a realistic reason to become involved in the investigation.

Since the victim does not exist in isolation, try to explore their relationships with other characters, both positive and negative. Friends, family, rivals, and acquaintances all play a role in shaping the victim's narrative. By introducing more layers to how the victim interacts with others, you begin to drop the breadcrumbs that will lead to the next part of our character list: the suspects.

Suspects: The Lineup of Potential Villains

Just as no two snowflakes are alike, no two suspects should be carbon copies of each other. Try to build your suspects in a similar fashion as you would your victim and add as much detail as you need to visualize them better. Consider their quirks, flaws, and hidden depths, painting them as multi-dimensional characters that defy easy categorization.

I find it helps tremendously to keep a file on every suspect I plan to have my sleuth interview. Think of yourself as a detective working a case—something your sleuth will soon become—and use these files as digital file folders. Each one should have the name of the suspect, their description, occupation, background, known feuds, known allies, etc. The more detail you have, the better. As always, not all of this information will end up on the page, but it will be much easier for you to write these people if you know them inside and out.

You can use the following as guides to creating your suspect "folders".

Suspect Criminal File

Suspect's Name and Physical Description:

- Full Name
- Height

- Build
- Hair Color/Style
- Eye Color
- Distinguishing Features

Background Information:

- Occupation
- Education
- Family
- Residency

Alibi:

- Where were they at the time of the crime?
- Who can verify their whereabouts?
- Any evidence supporting their alibi?

Relationship with Victim:

- How did they know the victim?
- Any conflicts or disagreements?
- Past interactions or history?

Motive:

- Did they have any reason to harm the victim?
- Financial, personal, or professional motives?
- Any prior incidents suggesting motive?

Behavior on the Day of the Crime:

- What were they doing before, during, and after the crime?
- Any suspicious behavior or actions?

Witness Testimonies:

- Any witnesses who saw the suspect around the time of the crime?
- What did they observe about the suspect's behavior?

Evidence:

- Any physical evidence linking the suspect to the crime scene?
- Fingerprints, DNA, personal belongings, etc.

When formulating your list of suspects,

remember that in these close-knit communities, every character hides something—be it a harmless quirk or a dark deed waiting to be uncovered. These secrets serve as the fuel that ignites the mystery, providing both motive and opportunity for the crime at hand.

Just as the suspects are interconnected with the victim, they are also intertwined with each other. Consider the relationships and dynamics that exist within the community, from old grudges to hidden alliances. Each suspect should have a unique relationship with the victim and other suspects, creating a tangled web of motives and opportunities. We will go into more detail on how to manufacture a complicated web of connections in later chapters, but I want you to start thinking about where your suspects fit in the community as you begin to design your cast.

The suspects in a cozy mystery play an active role in driving the narrative forward. As the investigation progresses, they may grow increasingly desperate, resorting to dire measures to protect themselves or frame others. Their actions and reactions add layers of complexity to the mystery, keeping both the sleuth and the reader on their toes.

And with that, your list of characters is complete. By now, you should have your sleuth, the villain, a victim (or two), your suspects, and the supporting cast. A lot of people to keep track of!

Since we have such a growing population of characters, it's high time we moved onto the next important part of the cozy mystery novel. Our characters need somewhere to live. Join me in the next part to build the world your mystery belongs to by creating a setting that your readers will wish they could visit.

PART 2
CREATING SETTINGS

CHAPTER 7

Developing a Cozy Setting

The place where your cozy mystery is set becomes almost a character of its own. Readers expect to be pulled into a space that is all enveloping and one that they can truly sink their teeth into. Your job, dear writer, is to make sure that the reader can visualize the setting of your story in every detail. From the sights, to the smells, to the way the rain sounds on the rooftops of local shops—nothing can be left to chance.

When I was first creating Orchard Hollow, I went through multiple iterations of the town. The first was not small enough to form a tight-knit community. The second version was much too big and gave my sleuth no chance of solving the clues in a timely matter. There were several more that didn't quite fit. Are we starting to see a pattern here? When working out your setting, you too might feel like Goldilocks and the three bears. But trust me when I tell you, your setting will pull itself together.

When beginning to craft your setting, there are a few things to consider.

Setting the Stage

Before you even put pen to paper (or fingers to keyboard), take some time to think about where the location of your mystery will be set. Will it be a cute village, a tourist-filled small town, or a charming spot on the coast? The setting you choose will not only influence the tone of your story, but also shape the dynamics between your characters and the type of mysteries they encounter.

It might even give you ideas on how to structure the dialect for your characters or help progress through a series of books.

Actionable Tip:

- If writing a historical mystery, try to watch many movies set in the same timeline. These don't have to be mysteries but should have a good representation of the era to give you a better idea of how to portray it well.

This tip actually takes me to my next point—do your research!

Research and Inspiration

Drawing inspiration from real-life locations can add a level of realism to your setting. Whether it's a shop you stumbled upon during a weekend getaway or the historic mansion you've always wanted to visit, incorporating elements of real places into your setting can help bring it to life for your readers.

I like to take a million photos when I am out and about, especially when on vacation, because I find they always help in creating an atmosphere when I am reaching for ideas. My most recent cozy mystery (as of writing this book) is set on a tropical island that is based on a location we love to visit as a family. I loved it so much I sent my sleuth there too!

Actionable Tip:

- Pay attention to architectural details, local customs, and regional dialects that can lend authenticity to your descriptions. Consider incorporating specific landmarks or points of interest that add depth to the setting, making it feel like a place readers could visit themselves.

Creating a Sense of Place

Once you've chosen your setting, it's time to bring it to life with your words. As I mentioned above, describe the sights, sounds, and smells that make your setting unique. Is it the scent of freshly baked bread wafting from the local bakery? The sound of seagulls circling overhead while waves crash against the cliffs? Paying attention to these sensory details will help transport your readers into the heart of your story and make them feel like they're right there alongside your characters.

Actionable Tip:

- Find a space that is close to the one that you are trying to describe and spend some time there. Bring an audio recorder or use a recording app on your phone to get even more details you can use later. If you are a decent artist, sketch out the place in your notebook or snap some photos instead.

Establishing Atmosphere

Atmosphere is key to creating a cozy mystery that draws readers in and keeps them hooked until the very end. Whether you're writing a humorous mystery or one that has darker undertones, your setting should reflect the mood you're trying to convey. Use weather, time of day, and the surrounding environment to set the tone for each scene. A foggy morning might lend an air of gloom to your story, while a sunny picnic could signal a moment of peace and quiet before the next clue drops.

Actionable Tip:

- To develop the atmosphere of your setting, focus on descriptive details that appeal to the senses. The more details you can provide, the better.

Using Setting to Enhance Plot

In a cozy mystery, the setting isn't just a backdrop—it's an integral part of the plot. Use your setting to your advantage by incorporating elements that help drive the story forward. Depending on where you set your mystery, there could be places that help with planting clues or leading your sleuth astray.

When thinking of the geography of your setting, try to imagine your sleuth walking along the streets and take note of what they would see. Small hidden spaces are great to hide secrets in. In the same vein, try to use your setting to help you plan out your antagonist's next moves.

I find it helps to draw a rough map of the town and locations my stories take place in. You don't have to be an artist to do this, but if you're a perfectionist like me, there are programs online that are amazing for map drawing.

Actionable Tip:

- Once you have the plot of your cozy mystery, read through it and see where you can highlight the setting of your novel more. If you find that your plot does not include the setting enough, try to add scenes where you can explore the area in more detail by the actions of your sleuth and supporting cast.

Evoking Nostalgia and Comfort

At its core, the cozy mystery genre is all about nostalgia and comfort. Cozy is quite literally in the name! With that in mind, your setting should reflect a sense of familiarity and a space where the reader can kick their shoes off and relax.

Actionable Tip:

- Keep a Pinterest Board with all the cozy images you can find. Devote a short amount of time daily before you start plotting your novel to looking for images to add to the board. Once you start writing, pull this board up and keep it somewhere you can see it so you always have the cozy feeling of your setting at the front of your mind. I make mood boards with images that help me visual my towns and the spaces within them.

Which brings me to my last point. Your setting is not limited to the geographical location where your story takes place. A setting can be anything from a busy street where you get shoulder-checked trying to walk from one place to the next, to a small reading nook in a local library. Don't fall into the trap of over-describing your main spaces and forgetting about the ones that don't seem to play a big part in the story. In order to engage your reader in your setting, you have to show it to them in the same way they would see a movie. The more emotions you can evoke, the more they will immerse themselves in your setting and never want to leave.

Are you ready to start thinking about the setting of your mystery? Grab a pen and paper and let's get started! You will find some prompts in the next section that you can use to start building out your setting. When you're done constructing your cozy fictional world, it will be time to move onto the main event—the plot of your cozy mystery.

COZY SETTING DEVELOPMENT

1. Setting Description:

- Name of Town/Village:
- Location (e.g., countryside, coastal, mountains):
- Climate:
- Size and Population:
- Notable Landmarks or Points of Interest:

2. Atmosphere and Mood:

- Describe the overall atmosphere of the setting (e.g., cozy, charming, quirky).
- What mood do you want to evoke in your readers (e.g., nostalgia, warmth, suspense)?

3. Unique Features:

- Identify the distinctive characteristics that set your setting apart from others (e.g.,

historic buildings, local festivals, natural wonders).
- How do these features contribute to the charm and appeal of the setting?

4. Local Businesses and Establishments:

- List the shops, restaurants, and businesses that populate your setting.
- Describe their specialties, ambiance, and any unique quirks or eccentricities.

5. Community Dynamics:

- Explore the social dynamics within the community (e.g., tight-knit, gossip-prone, welcoming to outsiders).
- What roles do local residents play in the fabric of the community (e.g., town elders, busybodies, beloved figures)?

6. Seasonal Changes:

- How does the setting change throughout the seasons?
- Describe the seasonal activities, events,

and traditions that shape life in the community.

7. Secrets and Intrigues:

- What hidden secrets or mysteries lurk beneath the surface of your setting?
- How do these secrets impact the lives of the residents and drive the plot of your mystery?

8. Setting-Character Interaction:

- How do the features of the setting influence the behavior and interactions of your characters?
- In what ways does the setting become a character in its own right, shaping the events of the story?

9. Reader Engagement:

- Consider how you can make your setting come alive for readers.
- How can you use descriptive language and sensory details to immerse readers in

the sights, sounds, and smells of your setting?

PART 3
OUTLINE AND PLOT

CONSTRUCTING AN ENGAGING PLOT

Thinking about characters and the world they will live in is incredibly fun and an insightful exercise to partake in. But what is a novel without a plot? If you have been following me online or watching my YouTube channel (something I encourage you to do since I share a lot of tips there), you will know that I am very much a plotter. However, it is also possible to write a cozy mystery if you're a pantser. The rules are different for everyone and there is no one right way to develop a story. I will recommend that no matter how much you enjoy outlining that you give your story a good think through before committing to putting words on the page.

The reason for this is because of the web you will need to spin in order to create a complicated, twisty, and interesting mystery for your readers. I don't know about you, but I have trouble keeping all the information in my head, especially when I am writing a series that consists of many books. Which is where the plotting part of writing a cozy comes in.

You might be excited for this part or you might be weary of getting started. Wherever you fall, I promise that by the time you're done with this section of the book, you will have a better idea of the center of your book: the mystery itself.

As you read through the following chapters, you will see me use terms such as acts and beats, as well as some other terminology that might be new to you if this is your first book. I will explain part of the cozy mystery plot in detail but for now, you should know that we will be using the four-act structure to outline our cozy mystery. It is the plotting structure I use myself and the one I find is best tailored to the genre. At the end of the plotting section, I have included several resources for you to use as you work on outlining your story.

The first resource you will receive is a beat sheet with detailed instructions on what each beat (or scene) should include and where they fall in the structure of the four acts. You can use this beat sheet as is or tailor it to fit your needs. As I mentioned before, there is no right or wrong way. Whatever helps you get the story on the page is what you should use.

The next resource is a crime brainstorm that has questions to think about when planning out the crime to be committed. Some parts we have already gone through when we created our characters so feel free to move the information over as you see fit.

Finally, you will receive a sample Author Murder Board which is exactly what it sounds like. This is a system I use myself to weave in the intricate overlapping connections between the suspects and the victim. Using this board will help you create the spiderweb of mystery, similar to the ones you see in detective movies. The difference is that ours will be handwritten on the page and not a massive board with red strings criss-crossing, because who has the space for that?

The most important thing to remember as you read the upcoming chapters is that nothing is set in stone. The plot of your book may change considerably as you begin to write and that's all right. When I plot, I leave space for the story to naturally evolve. Your characters will often move in a different way than you originally expected and I want you not to put too much pressure on yourself if that happens. Follow them and see where things lead. For me, I often discover toward the third act that the villain is not the one I originally anticipated, or that they didn't act alone. I love this part of writing! The reason being that if something catches me by surprise, chances are it will do the same to my readers.

Let your story guide and inspire you and you never know, you might discover a twist in the process that you never imagined.

Now if you're ready, dear writer, I'd like to start right in the action and tell you all about the four-act structure and how you can use it to write a cozy mystery your readers will devour.

CHAPTER 8

Four-act Structure

The four-act structure is a framework to divide the narrative of your story in a way that guides the reader along the plot. Much like other plotting systems, this method has beats and points in the story outline that fall into specific acts and sections of the plot. In case you're not familiar with the term of a beat, it is essentially a scene that you will write.

The acts themselves are close to what one would see in theater, with each one serving a purpose in the development of the story. The four-act structure is close to the three-act structure, but it introduces another act in the middle to divide the plot into four distinct parts. The way I like to think of it is while in a three-act structure, your second act is the longest. In the four-act structure, that act gets sliced in half to make two.

You will see what I mean as we get into the

breakdown of each one below and in the beat sheet I have provided at the end of this section of the book.

If you're wondering why this is the structure I recommend and use myself when outlining cozy mysteries, it is because the division of the acts works well in the narrative of a mystery. You get enough time to set up the story and introduce the mystery, two full acts for investigation, and a final section where you can bring the entire story to a close. In my opinion, the four-act structure is the perfect narrative template for cozies.

Let's see what each act in the structure consists of, so you can see why it is such a great fit for our purposes.

Act 1: Setup

The first act establishes the setting, introduces the main characters, and sets up the central mystery or problem. In cozy mysteries, this often involves introducing the amateur sleuth, the close-knit community where the story takes place, and the initial crime or puzzle that needs solving. This act sets the stage for the rest of the story, drawing readers into the world of the mystery and laying the groundwork for the investigation to come.

In the introductory act of the story, we get to

connect to the sleuth and get to know their surroundings. With such, we instantly form a relationship so that when the crime happens, we have skin in the game alongside the sleuth. This is also the act where the writer often hints at something amiss and gives foreshadowing at the crime to come.

Now this next opinion varies, but I like to introduce the crime earlier in the first act and end the act with the sleuth being thrown into the investigation. Some writers close out the act with the murder, but I feel that for my cozies, the crime happening before the end of act one tends to lock in the reader more deeply. I use the crime as a starting point to convince the reader why the sleuth must investigate what happened. They might be reluctant at first, but something always happens in the first act that makes it impossible for them not to move forward.

Perhaps they are implicated in the crime or someone they care about is in danger. Whatever the reason is, I end my first acts with the sleuth taking the first step forward in solving the mystery.

In Devil in a French Press, Piper makes a decision to investigate the death of a fellow witch after her mother convinces her it is the only choice they have. If they do not throw the town's sheriff off track, his life, and the life of other humans will be in grave danger. With this decision, the act ends, and the reader must continue forward to see what happens next.

Act 2: Complications

In the second act, complications arise as the amateur sleuth digs deeper into the mystery. This is where red herrings, false leads, and unexpected twists come into play. The sleuth encounters obstacles and challenges that make solving the mystery more difficult, and the tension begins to build as the stakes are raised. Cozy mysteries often feature a mix of humor, wit, and intrigue during this act, as the amateur sleuth navigates the eccentricities of the community and uncovers secrets hidden beneath the surface.

During the progression of the act, the reader is taken on a wild ride of theories as the sleuth tries to piece together the puzzle. They, of course, fail since there are so many missing pieces and you, as the writer, keep throwing obstacles in their way.

If you have a sub-plot, the second act is where it will get page time. We want to avoid adding sub-plots into the first act so we can concentrate on the main mystery. The one exception to this would be a romantic sub-plot where we can meet the romantic interest. However, even after meeting them, I would refrain from following up on that sub-plot until the second act, where we have more space to develop it properly and give it room to breathe.

The second act will almost always end with a midpoint, which more often than not includes a second crime. If you have a murder as a central mystery, the midpoint is where you have the chance to get rid of your sleuth's lead suspect, thus throwing them off course.

Act 3: Climax

The climax, or act three, is the pivotal moment in the story where the pieces of the puzzle start to come together. The amateur sleuth, armed with new clues and theories, confronts the suspects and discovers the truth behind the mystery. This act is characterized by heightened tension and suspense as the stakes reach their peak and the final showdown between the sleuth and the villain unfolds. In cozy mysteries, the climax often combines a race against time to solve the case before it's too late.

During the third act, the sleuth will be narrowing down the suspect pool via a second round of investigations. We want to make sure that these don't drag on. When working on this act, try to make each of your chapters incorporate some form of action.

Essentially, the third act is all about doing and not about talking.

If your sleuth has special skills, this is where they will use them to their top advantage. As the stakes rise and the villain continues to attack and throw the sleuth off track, they need to make use of their entire arsenal of abilities to stop them. Alternatively, this could also be the act where your sleuth discovers new skills that will help them solve the crime.

The third act comes to a close on a pivotal low moment for our amateur sleuth. This could be the moment the antagonist does something that makes them feel like they can never get ahead or it could be that the sleuth is losing confidence in their own abilities. The low point has to feel like the absolute end and the reader has to be right there with your sleuth in the gutter.

When I was writing *Killing Grinds*, I wanted to make sure that the third act made Piper believe she hit a final dead end. Since this investigation was especially close to her heart as it involved the mysterious death of her ghost familiar, the dead end had to make our sleuth crumble. After encountering multiple barriers, Piper got a call from the town sheriff letting her know that the only suspect she had was found dead. This was a deliberate choice I made to add another murder this late in the book, but it worked out well. Piper was distraught and the readers couldn't wait to see how she was going to get out of this terrible predicament. Sometimes placing the second crime in a spot the reader doesn't expect pays off so feel free to experiment with your beats as you become more comfortable writing in the genre.

Act 4: Resolution

The fourth act provides closure and resolution to the story. With the mystery solved and the culprit apprehended, loose ends are tied up, and the community returns to a state of equilibrium. Cozy mysteries typically end on a satisfying note, with justice served and the amateur sleuth celebrated for their help and perseverance. This act may also hint at future adventures or developments for the protagonist, setting the stage for the next installments in a series.

But before we get to the celebration, we must help our sleuth to apprehend the villain. Having reached a low point at the end of act three, they need a little push to get back up and keep on fighting. To put it in terms a lot will understand, this is their Rocky moment. No matter how hard they may have gotten hit, they need to move forward. To do so, your sleuth must rise from the ashes and formulate a new plan—they will defeat the villain!

Since this is a cozy mystery, emphasis on cozy, the final battle cannot be gory or overly horrific. At times, it helps to add humor to the defeat of the villain as it can help the reader come to terms with the finality of the act. In my book Six Brews Under, I used a herd of iguanas to help apprehend the villains. That's right, you heard correctly. The creatures were indigenous to the island Piper was on and I made sure to add plenty of mentions of them throughout so that when we got to the resolution of act four, the reader could laugh along at the absurdity of the situation.

Try to end the fourth act on a positive note. The final chapter of your cozy mystery is a good time to tie off loose ends. We want to show our amateur sleuth in a happy place, the villain behind bars, and the community once again safe from crime and mischief.

Now that we have covered what the four-act structure is and how you can use it to better outline your cozy mystery, I hope you feel emboldened to move forward. Take out a large piece of paper and divide it into four, then make some notes on each act as you brainstorm the main plot points of your mystery. When you're done, use the provided beat breakdown to narrow the plot down further. I use a combination of tools to help me with this part, starting with notecards and ending with a digital version of my final plot on the computer. Pick a system of note-taking that works for you and don't worry about changing it up from book to book. Making these changes helps with our creativity.

With the structure of the cozy mystery covered, I'd like to move on to another very important piece of the genre: the importance of the puzzle. The puzzle is what the reader is here for. Let's use the next chapter of the book to go over how you can create a mystery that keeps your sleuth and your readers guessing until the very end.

CHAPTER 9

The Importance of the Puzzle

When I think about a cozy mystery, or mystery of any kind, the first thing that comes to mind is the puzzle. After all, it is what the readers are here for, to try to out-sleuth the sleuth. Because it plays such an important part, the puzzle is one of the things you should spend the most time on. You want to think about it for a while, let it sit, come back to think about it again.

If you are a pantser, this is the only part of the novel that I always recommend you take the time to outline. While you can wing your way through it, there is a very good chance you'll write yourself into a hole if you don't plan ahead. Or worse, create a puzzle that is too easy to solve.

When thinking of the puzzle for your sleuth to figure out, there several factors to consider.

The Intrigue of the Unsolved

At the core of every cozy lies the allure of the unsolved puzzle—a mystery waiting to be deciphered. Readers are drawn to the challenge of unraveling it, eagerly poring over clues and piecing together fragments of evidence as they join your sleuth in their investigation. The key to crafting a compelling puzzle lies in striking the perfect balance between intrigue and solvability, leaving readers guessing until the very end.

With that said, you want to avoid solving the mystery with something that comes out of the blue. Everyone loves a good twist, but the surprise shouldn't be so shocking that the reader feels it comes out of left field. You must find a balance between complexity and well-delivered clues.

Which brings me to my next point.

Creating Complexity

To craft a puzzle that truly stumps readers, you should rely on complicated webs of deceit. Layering clues upon clues, weaving together deception and misdirection, challenges readers to think critically and consider every possibility. Red herrings, those fun distractions that lead readers astray, play a crucial role in keeping the puzzle alive. If you are not familiar with the term, the red herring is used to note a false clue. The term was coined in the early 19th century. Its origin is often attributed to the practice of using a smoked, strong-smelling fish, typically a herring, to train hunting dogs to follow a scent. Trainers would drag the fish across the trail they wanted the dogs to follow. Eventually, however, the term evolved to describe a deliberate distraction, or in our case, misdirection.

A lot of times you will use suspects as red herrings, placing heavy doubt on another character to distract from the real villain. Keep in mind, your villain can also employ red herrings to get away with their crime. By planting false trails and sowing seeds of doubt, you can ensure that the journey to the truth is anything but straightforward.

To get a well-crafted complex puzzle, use the Author Murder Board provided to add intertwined relationships between your suspects. The more you can make your sleuth run around searching, the more you will confuse the reader as well.

Misdirection is a powerful tool in the arsenal of any mystery writer—a means of leading readers down unexpected paths and keeping them on their toes. Whether it's a plot twist or a cleverly placed red herring, misdirection keeps readers guessing and ensures that the puzzle remains unsolved until the very last moment. But like any tool, be careful not to overuse it so you don't end up frustrating your reader.

Adding Clues and Breadcrumbs

When it comes to cozy mysteries, every detail matters—every seemingly innocuous clue or offhand remark holds the potential to solving the crime and finding out the villain. By scattering clues like breadcrumbs throughout the narrative, you guide your readers on a trail, leading them ever closer to the solution. Much like Hansel and Gretel traveling into the depths of the forest in search of a candy house, our reader should be following the crumbs you leave behind into the belly of the mystery.

I find the best way to do this is to plot your story first, then pepper in the clues after. You can always add more clues during the editing phase, which is how I personally enjoy working. Consider using conversation and description of places when you are adding your clues. Even something as simple as a smell noted by your sleuth or a supporting cast member can make the reader intrinsically catch on.

It is these details that cozy mystery readers crave. Make sure you take the time to load your book up with well-hidden Easter Eggs for them to search for. After all, the witch house is hidden deep in the forest for a reason...

The Satisfaction of Solving the Puzzle

The one thing that all readers of cozies look for is the promise of satisfaction—a moment of clarity when the puzzle is finally solved. It is a time of triumph for both reader and sleuth alike, as the pieces of the mystery fall into place and the truth is revealed. But the way they get to this moment is just as important as the destination itself, for it is the challenges faced along the way that make the victory so sweet.

As you work on your mystery, build up to that final moment at a slow pace. Use it as a crescendo in a symphony, the big blast of notes at the end that makes the crowd stand up and clap. When your sleuth has their final realization, your reader should be itching to flip back through the pages to see what they may have missed. Do you see now how all those clues and misdirections play a pivotal role?

One great way to add more meat to your puzzle is to weave in sub-plots. These can help redirect the reader's attention while you cleverly plant clues for them to miss throughout the book. But adding subplots in a seamless manner can be an art onto itself, which is why I'd like to take the time to discuss it further in the following chapter.

CHAPTER 10

Weaving In Subplots

In order to properly write subplots into your story, we must first understand what a subplot is.

A subplot is a secondary storyline that runs parallel to the main plot. While the central plot focuses on the central conflict and primary characters, a subplot introduces additional characters, conflicts, or themes that enrich the story. Subplots often intersect with the central plot, influencing its development or providing contrast, but they can also stand on their own to offer depth and complexity to the narrative. They may serve various purposes, such as character development, thematic exploration, or providing comic relief.

In layman's terms, it is a plot but much smaller in scope. While your subplots can have arching storylines and require forward momentum through the story, they will not have as much depth and detail as the main plot of your cozy. If you are, however, writing a longer series, you can play with weaving in a subplot that stretches for the duration of the books. With that said, the central plot of your story has to wrap up in each book and those mysteries must get solved before moving on.

There are many types of subplots you can play around with when developing your mystery. Let's take a look at some of the more common subplots and themes to help you decide on which direction you'd like to go with in your book.

Character-driven Subplots

These subplots explore the lives of your characters beyond the central mystery by tapping into their personal struggles, relationships, and big internal goals. Each of the characters in your book, sleuth, villain, and supporting cast, can bring their own subplots to the table. By weaving in secondary stories from other characters, you give your reader a deeper look into the world you're building and help to keep their interest beyond the main mystery.

Consider the hobbies, occupations, or interests of your characters as potential sources of subplot material. Whether it's a new romance, a longstanding rivalry, or a hidden talent, these personal arcs can add layers of interest to your narrative.

In Orchard Hollow, I use Piper's malfunctioning

magic as a subplot to help drive the story of her relationship with her mother across the series. As the reader gets deeper into the books, more secrets are unveiled as we build up to the final resolution of the subplot. To make the subplot more satisfactory, I dedicated the final book in the series to the solving of its mystery.

Parallel Investigations

Introduce parallel investigations or secondary mysteries that run alongside the main plot. These subplots can involve different characters, settings, or even time periods, offering readers a multifaceted view of the story world.

Use those investigations to add new views to the central mystery or to introduce new clues and suspects. By intertwining these subplots with the main narrative, you can keep readers engaged and guessing until the very end.

A good idea for a parallel investigation is a crime that may have occurred years before the current mystery but is related somehow. I used the parallel mystery of a previous death to drive the plot of A Grave Roast forward. As my sleuth investigated, it became apparent that the two murders were not only connected, but were committed by the same villain.

Because of this, the solving of the crime was that much more juicy for the readers.

Community Dynamics

When writing, look into the dynamics within the community where the mystery occurs by introducing subplots that involve interactions between various residents. This could include rivalries between local businesses, tensions among neighborhood associations, or longstanding feuds between families. You can even involve your sleuth into these subplots, especially if they have a business or hobby of their own that might interfere with that of another.

Choosing to use the community and supporting cast in your subplots will get your reader to fall in love with your world because they could picture themselves in it. One of the best compliments I received from my editor was for the book Six Brews Under. When outlining the book, I knew I wanted to paint the picture of an idyllic island that gets interrupted by a large developer taking over and building resorts on land that doesn't belong to him. I used this story in the subplot and even as a tool to throw shade onto a character—my red herring.

Unbeknownst to me, my editor happened to live in an area with very similar problems. One of her notes in the editorial letter was how much she could relate to the locals and their different levels of upset, and how it made her love the story more.

In this case, my subplot quite literally hooked a reader.

Past Secrets and Intrigues

Introduce subplots that uncover long-buried secrets that have ramifications in the present. These subplots could involve characters with hidden pasts, unsolved mysteries from years gone by, or scandals that refuse to stay buried.

Use flashbacks, journal entries, or other narrative devices to explore the backstory behind these past secrets, gradually revealing the truth as the main plot unfolds. By intertwining the past and present, you can create a sense of continuity and resonance that deepens the mystery.

This subplot relates to parallel investigations, but is more open-ended. A subplot with secrets can involve a past crime but is more directed at uncovering secrets and the dark past of the sleuth and the surrounding characters.

Family Matters

Using the sleuth's family as a subplot is a great way to make them more relatable in the eyes of your reader. This could include sibling rivalries, parental expectations, or generational conflicts that play out against the backdrop of the central mystery.

Use family-based subplots to add emotional depth and complexity to the characters in your book, revealing their vulnerabilities, fears, and desires.

By going down this route, you can create more complex character arcs for your sleuth, your villain, and all those in the cozy community they occupy. My choice to give Piper a complex relationship with her mother added tension to the series that it otherwise lacked and gave me a new plot to explore when her wayward mother returned in one of the books.

Personal Growth and Transformation

Chart the personal growth and transformation of your sleuth through subplots that challenge their beliefs, values, and priorities. This could include arcs focused on self-discovery, overcoming adversity, or finding redemption in the face of past mistakes.

If you're writing a paranormal cozy mystery, this type of subplot works very well alongside the discovery of magic. Your sleuth might be learning of their new powers, strengthening the ones they have, or finding out the truth of where their powers came from.

Resolution and Closure

Ensure that each subplot receives its own resolution and closure by the end of the book, or series, if you are using a subplot to carry it. Whether it's a character arc that comes full circle or a secondary mystery that is finally solved, tying up loose ends in your subplots helps readers feel like they didn't waste their time.

As I mentioned above, the main mystery of each one of the books in your series needs to wrap up in a tidy bow, and while the subplot can continue through the series, there also needs to be some resolution from book to book. Essentially, you want to give the reader just enough to feel satisfied, but keep the subplot open and provide a cliffhanger for the next story to come.

For example, the subplot of Stella's mysterious death in Orchard Hollow was hinted at for the first two books and not solved until book three. I did this in order to give the reader time to get personally invested in the ghost's death and to build up a desire for vindication. By the time we got to Killing Grinds, solving the crime became a personal matter for the readers.

Using subplots as a tool to drive the narrative is a great way to add tension and drama to your cozy mystery. Despite the subjects of cozies being on the lighter side, it doesn't mean that the reader won't expect a rollercoaster ride of a mystery. Subplots can help you get there.

In the pages ahead, you will find three tools I use all the time when outlining my cozy mysteries: the beat sheet, the crime brainstorm template, and the author murder board. Once you're done filling these out, I want to move right along and talk to you about the pacing of your story. In order to grip the reader and string them along, we need the pacing to be just right. Are you ready to build some tension?

COZY MYSTERY BEAT SHEET

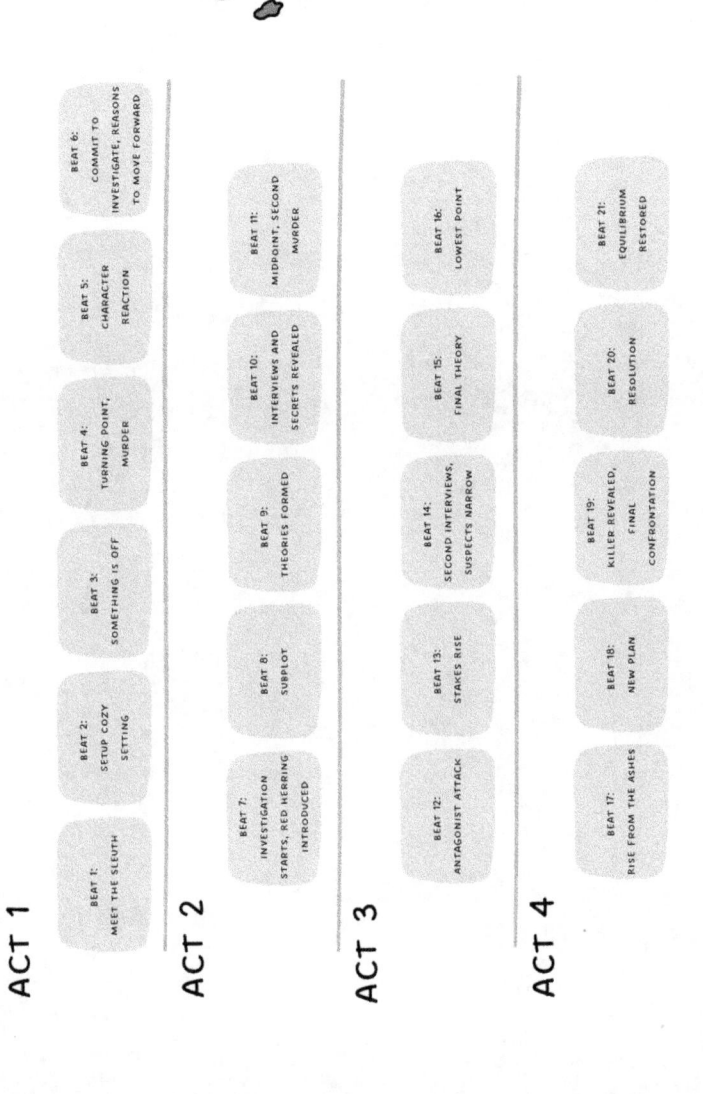

ACT 1
- BEAT 1: MEET THE SLEUTH
- BEAT 2: SETUP COZY SETTING
- BEAT 3: SOMETHING IS OFF
- BEAT 4: TURNING POINT, MURDER
- BEAT 5: CHARACTER REACTION
- BEAT 6: COMMIT TO INVESTIGATE, REASONS TO MOVE FORWARD

ACT 2
- BEAT 7: INVESTIGATION STARTS, RED HERRING INTRODUCED
- BEAT 8: SUBPLOT
- BEAT 9: THEORIES FORMED
- BEAT 10: INTERVIEWS AND SECRETS REVEALED
- BEAT 11: MIDPOINT, SECOND MURDER

ACT 3
- BEAT 12: ANTAGONIST ATTACK
- BEAT 13: STAKES RISE
- BEAT 14: SECOND INTERVIEWS, SUSPECTS NARROW
- BEAT 15: FINAL THEORY
- BEAT 16: LOWEST POINT

ACT 4
- BEAT 17: RISE FROM THE ASHES
- BEAT 18: NEW PLAN
- BEAT 19: KILLER REVEALED, FINAL CONFRONTATION
- BEAT 20: RESOLUTION
- BEAT 21: EQUILIBRIUM RESTORED

COZY MYSTERY BEAT BREAKDOWN

Act One

Beat 1: Meet the Sleuth

This is where readers are introduced to the main character, often the amateur sleuth, who will be navigating through the mystery. It's essential to establish their personality, quirks, and motivations early on to create a connection with the audience.

1. Background and Personality:

Start by defining who your sleuth is. What is their background? Are they an amateur detective, a professional investigator, or someone unexpectedly drawn into solving mysteries? Consider their age, occupation, hobbies, and any quirks or unique traits that make them interesting and relatable to readers.

2. Motivation for Solving Mysteries:

What motivates your sleuth to solve mysteries? Are they driven by a desire for justice, curiosity, or personal reasons? Understanding their motivations will help you shape their character arc and guide their actions throughout the story.

3. Strengths and Weaknesses:

Every sleuth should have strengths that aid them in solving mysteries, as well as weaknesses that present challenges and obstacles to overcome. These can be physical, intellectual, or emotional traits that add depth to the character and create opportunities for growth and development.

4. Relationships:

Look at the sleuth's relationships with other characters in the story. Do they have a sidekick, partner, or mentor who assists them in their investigations? What about friends, family members, or romantic interests? Developing these relationships can add complexity to the sleuth's character and provide opportunities for interesting interactions and subplots.

5. Setting Introduction:

Introduce your sleuth in their everyday environment, whether it's a small town, bustling city, or picturesque countryside. Show readers what their life is like before they become embroiled in the mystery, giving them a sense of the sleuth's daily routine, surroundings, and community.

6. First Impression:

Make sure the sleuth's introduction leaves a

strong impression on readers. This could involve showcasing their wit, intelligence, or knack for observation, as well as hinting at the challenges they will face in the upcoming mystery. Consider including a moment of intrigue or curiosity that draws readers in and makes them eager to follow the sleuth's journey.

7. Unique Skills or Talents:

Does your sleuth have any special skills or talents that make them particularly adept at solving mysteries? Whether it's a background in law enforcement, a talent for deciphering codes, or a keen eye for detail, highlighting these abilities can set your sleuth apart and provide opportunities for creative problem-solving in your story.

8. Sidekick:

If there is a sidekick or helper, this is the beat to introduce them in. Be it a furry one, a human one, or a paranormal creature for those magical cozies!

Beat 2: Setup Cozy Setting

The cozy mystery genre is known for its charming settings, often small towns or villages. This beat is all about immersing the reader in the cozy atmosphere, introducing key locations, and establishing the community dynamics.

1. Choose a Charming Location:

Select a quaint, picturesque setting that evokes a sense of coziness and charm. This could be a small village, a rural town, a seaside community, or any other idyllic location that lends itself to a cozy atmosphere. Consider incorporating unique features, such as historic buildings, local landmarks, or scenic landscapes to add depth and richness to the setting.

2. Establish a Sense of Community:

Populate your setting with a cast of engaging characters who contribute to the sense of community and camaraderie. This could include friendly neighbors, local shopkeepers, quirky residents, and other colorful personalities who bring the setting to life. Show interactions between characters that highlight the bonds of friendship, support, and mutual respect that exist within the community.

3. Create Cozy Spaces:

Describe cozy interiors that invite readers to imagine themselves curling up with a good book or enjoying a cup of tea by the fireplace. Emphasize the comforting details that make these spaces feel warm and inviting. Use sensory descriptions to evoke the sights, sounds, smells, and textures that contribute to the cozy ambiance.

4. Highlight Seasonal Elements:

Take advantage of the changing seasons to

enhance the cozy atmosphere of your setting. Use seasonal details to create a sense of time and place, as well as opportunities for seasonal activities and events that add richness to the setting.

5. Incorporate Quirky Traditions:

Add unique traditions, festivals, or rituals that reflect the character of the community. Whether it's an annual bake-off, a traditional holiday celebration, or a superstition passed down through generations, these elements add depth and authenticity to the setting.

6. Establish a Sense of Safety:

Despite the presence of a mystery to be solved, ensure that the setting feels safe and welcoming to readers. Emphasize the close-knit nature of the community, where neighbors look out for one another and crime is rare. This sense of safety serves as a contrast to the intrigue and suspense of the plot.

7. Balance Charm with Intrigue:

While it's important to create a cozy atmosphere, be sure to balance the charm and familiarity with elements of suspense. Hint at the darker undercurrents lurking beneath the surface of the seemingly idyllic setting. This contrast adds depth to the story and keeps readers engaged as they follow the sleuth to uncover the truth.

Beat 3: Something is Off

A subtle disturbance or unusual event occurs, hinting at the impending mystery. This could be a strange occurrence, a suspicious character, or a sense of unease that disrupts the tranquil setting.

1. Foreshadowing and Suspense:

From the outset, sprinkle subtle hints and clues that suggest all is not as it seems in the world. These could be small anomalies, strange occurrences, or unexplained behaviors exhibited by the residents of the community. Build suspense by gradually escalating these clues, leaving readers eager to uncover the truth behind the mystery.

2. Character Intrigues:

Study the complexities of the characters inhabiting your cozy setting, introducing secrets, conflicts, and hidden agendas that hint at underlying tensions. Develop relationships based on misunderstandings or simmering resentments, creating a web of interpersonal intrigues that provide potential suspects for the mystery.

3. Unsolved Mysteries:

Incorporate references to past events or unsolved mysteries that linger in the background, casting a shadow over the otherwise charming setting. These unresolved elements could resurface unexpectedly, intertwining with the central mystery and adding layers of complexity to the plot.

4. Eerie Atmosphere:

Infuse the setting with an undercurrent of unease or eeriness that contrasts with its outward charm. Describe eerie landscapes, mysterious noises in the night, or unsettling encounters with strangers that leave characters and readers alike feeling unsettled. This atmospheric tension heightens the sense of anticipation as the mystery unfolds.

5. Add Details:

Introduce details that seem out of place or discordant with the cozy atmosphere, signaling to readers that something is off. This could include neglected properties, abandoned buildings, or unusual artifacts with murky origins that pique the sleuth's curiosity and drive them to investigate further.

6. Community Secrets:

Explore the secrets and scandals hidden beneath the surface of the tight-knit community. Uncover long-buried secrets, illicit affairs, or activities that threaten to unravel the fabric of the community and expose its residents to danger.

7. Mysterious Incidents:

Pepper the sleuth's world with mysterious incidents or accidents that defy explanation, fueling speculation and suspicion among the residents. These incidents could range from minor pranks and petty thefts to more sinister acts of vandalism or sabotage that hint at a deeper conspiracy waiting to be solved.

Beat 4: Turning Point, Murder

The central event that propels the story forward: the discovery of a murder. This is the catalyst that disrupts the peaceful setting and thrusts the sleuth into action.

1. Discovery of the Body:

Describe the moment when the body is discovered, setting the stage for shock and disbelief among the residents of the story. This could occur in a picturesque location—a scenic park, a charming bed-and-breakfast, or a village square—adding a layer of irony to the grim discovery.

2. Initial Suspicion:

Study the initial reactions of the characters to the murder, including shock, fear, and suspicion. Rumors and gossip may swirl as residents speculate about the identity of the victim and the motive behind the crime. Heighten the tension by revealing conflicting accounts and hidden agendas among the suspects, leaving readers guessing as to who might be responsible.

3. Sleuth's Involvement:

Establish the sleuth's connection to the murder and their motivations for getting involved in the investigation. This could be personal—such as a friendship or familial tie to the victim—or driven by a sense of justice and a desire to uncover the truth. Use the turning point to propel the sleuth into action, setting them on a collision course with danger as they dig deeper into the mystery.

4. Police Investigation:

Introduce the local law enforcement officials responsible for investigating the murder, portraying them as competent professionals who take the crime seriously. However, also highlight their limitations and potential blind spots, leaving room for the amateur sleuth to make their own discoveries and contributions to the investigation.

5. Clues and Red Herrings:

Scatter clues and red herrings throughout the story, leading both the sleuth and the readers on a twisting path of investigation. These clues could be physical evidence, eyewitness accounts, or seemingly innocuous details that take on new significance as the story unfolds. Keep readers guessing by introducing false leads and misdirection, challenging them to separate fact from fiction.

6. Motive and Suspects:

Introduce the potential motives and suspects behind the murder, weaving in suspicion around the residents. Dig into the characters' backstories, relationships, and secrets, revealing hidden tensions and rivalries that provide plausible motives for the crime. Keep readers engaged by introducing a diverse cast of suspects with compelling reasons to be both guilty and innocent.

7. Impact on the Community:

Illustrate the ripple effect of the murder on the community, portraying the emotional aftermath and the ways in which residents come together—or fall apart—in the wake of the tragedy. Show how the crime disrupts the tranquility of the cozy setting, forcing characters to confront uncomfortable truths and grapple with their own vulnerabilities.

Beat 5: Character Reaction

The characters, especially the sleuth and those close to the victim, react to the murder. Emotions run high as shock and grief ripple through the community, setting the stage for the investigation to unfold.

1. Initial Shock and Disbelief:

Describe the sleuth's initial reaction to the discovery of the murder, capturing their shock and disbelief at the grisly scene before them. This could manifest as a physical reaction—such as a gasp of horror or a feeling of nausea—or an emotional one, as they struggle to process the reality of what they've stumbled upon.

2. Curiosity and Intrigue:

Explore the sleuth's natural curiosity and instinct to uncover the truth, which compels them to burrow deeper into the mystery despite the risks involved. This could stem from a sense of justice, a desire for closure, or simply a fascination with puzzles and riddles. Highlight the sleuth's determination to unravel the secrets hidden within the setting, even as they face resistance from those who would prefer the truth to remain buried.

3. Personal Connection to the Victim:

Establish any personal connection between the sleuth and the victim that motivates their involvement in the investigation. This could be a friendship, a familial tie, or a shared history that imbues the sleuth with a sense of obligation to seek justice on behalf of the victim. Use this connection to deepen the sleuth's emotional investment in solving the crime and heighten the stakes of their investigation.

4. Analytical Approach:

Showcase the sleuth's analytical skills and keen powers of observation as they begin to piece together the clues surrounding the murder. This could involve methodically collecting evidence and reconstructing the events leading up to the crime. Highlight the sleuth's attention to detail and knack for spotting inconsistencies or discrepancies that others might overlook, establishing them as a formidable amateur detective.

5. Emotional Turmoil:

Explore the sleuth's emotional turmoil as they grapple with the gravity of the situation and the risks involved in pursuing the truth. They may experience moments of fear, doubt, and vulnerability as they navigate the investigation, facing threats and obstacles that test their resolve. Show how the murder shakes the sleuth's sense of security and forces them to confront their own mortality.

6. Growing Resolve:

Show how the sleuth's reaction to the murder evolves over the course of the act, from initial shock and uncertainty to growing resolve and determination.

Beat 6: Commit to Investigate, Reasons to Move Forward

The sleuth makes a conscious decision to solve the mystery, driven by personal reasons, a sense of justice, or sheer curiosity. Motivations are established, and the stakes are set as the protagonist commits to uncovering the truth.

1. Sense of Duty:

Establish a sense of duty that compels the sleuth to move forward with the investigation. This could stem from their belief in justice, a desire to protect their community, or a personal connection to the victim. Highlight the sleuth's moral compass and their unwavering commitment to uncovering the truth, even in the face of danger or opposition.

2. Personal Stakes:

Establish personal stakes for the sleuth that motivate them to move forward with the investigation. This could involve threats to their safety or reputation, challenges to their credibility as an amateur detective, or unresolved issues from their past that resurface. Show how the murder impacts the sleuth on a personal level, heightening their emotional investment in solving the crime and driving their determination to see justice served.

3. Search for Closure:

Show the sleuth grapple with the aftermath of the murder. This could involve unresolved emotions, lingering questions, or a need for resolution that drives them to seek answers. Show how the sleuth's search for closure extends beyond their own personal motivations to encompass a broader desire to bring peace to the victim's loved ones and the community at large.

4. Desire for Redemption:

Illustrate the sleuth's desire for redemption as they confront their own shortcomings and mistakes. This could involve past failures, regrets, or missed opportunities that haunt the sleuth and drive them to make amends by solving the murder. Show how the sleuth's journey toward redemption is intertwined with their quest for justice.

5. Bond with Sidekick or Allies:

Highlight the bond between the sleuth and their sidekick, allies, or other members of the community who support them in their investigation. This could involve friends, family members, or fellow amateur detectives who offer guidance, assistance, or moral support as the sleuth navigates the twists and turns of the mystery. Show how these relationships strengthen the sleuth's resolve and provide a sense of camaraderie that bolsters their determination to see the investigation through to the end.

6. Sense of Responsibility to the Community:

Emphasize the sleuth's sense of responsibility to the community and their commitment to protecting others from harm by uncovering the truth behind the crime. Show how the sleuth's actions have far-reaching consequences that extend beyond their own personal interests, affecting the lives of those around them. By highlighting the broader implications of the murder and the sleuth's role in solving it, you can underscore the importance of their commitment to investigate and provide readers with a compelling reason to root for their success.

Act Two

Beat 7: Investigation Starts, Red Herring introduced

The sleuth begins their investigation, gathering clues and questioning suspects. Red herrings are introduced to throw both the sleuth and the reader off track, adding layers of complexity to the mystery.

1. Gathering Clues:

Show the sleuth actively gathering clues and evidence related to the crime. This could involve interviewing witnesses, examining the crime scene, and analyzing physical evidence, such as fingerprints or bloodstains. Highlight the sleuth's attention to detail and keen powers of observation as they methodically piece together the puzzle.

2. Initial Motives:

Dissect the motives of potential suspects, shedding light on their relationships with the victim and possible reasons for wanting them dead. Look at themes of jealousy, greed, revenge, and betrayal, to add suspicion around the characters. Show how each suspect has a plausible motive for the murder, complicating the sleuth's investigation and keeping readers guessing as to their true intentions.

3. Establishing Alibis:

Verify alibis and timelines for each suspect, corroborating their whereabouts at the time of the murder to eliminate false leads and narrow down the list of potential suspects. Highlight discrepancies or inconsistencies in their stories that raise doubts about their innocence. Keep readers on their toes by introducing red herrings—false clues or misleading information—that divert attention away from the true culprit and add complexity to the investigation.

4. Following Leads:

Follow leads and pursue avenues of inquiry that lead the sleuth closer to uncovering the truth behind the murder. This could involve connections between the victim and other characters, uncovering hidden secrets and scandals, or getting involved in a larger conspiracy. Use the investigation as an opportunity to reveal new clues.

5. Increasing Tension:

Raise the stakes of the investigation as the sleuth encounters obstacles and setbacks that threaten to derail their progress. This could involve threats to their safety, interference from powerful figures with something to hide, or unexpected twists and turns that lead the investigation in unexpected directions. Heighten the tension by ratcheting up the pressure on the sleuth to solve the murder before it's too late, adding urgency and excitement to the narrative as the story reaches its climax.

6. Building Suspense:

Build suspense as the sleuth closes in on the truth behind the murder, revealing shocking revelations and unexpected twists that challenge everything they thought they knew about the case. Use the introduction of the red herring to sow doubt and uncertainty in the sleuth's mind, forcing them to re-evaluate their assumptions and reconsider their suspects. Keep readers guessing until the very end as they eagerly anticipate the resolution of the mystery and the unmasking of the true culprit lurking within the story.

Beat 8: Subplot

While the focus remains on solving the murder, a

subplot emerges, adding to the story and developing secondary characters. This subplot often intertwines with the central mystery, providing additional twists and turns along the way.

1. Character Development:

Use the subplot to further develop the main characters. This could involve romantic entanglements, family drama, or career aspirations that intersect with the sleuth's investigation and impact their decisions and actions throughout the story.

2. Sidekick's Storyline:

Shine a spotlight on the sidekick or supporting characters by weaving their own storyline into the narrative. This could involve a personal dilemma, a secret past, or a hidden agenda that adds depth and complexity to their character while providing opportunities for them to contribute to the sleuth's investigation in unexpected ways.

3. Community Events:

Incorporate a subplot centered around a community event or tradition that intersects with the central mystery.

4. Personal Growth:

Use the subplot to chart the sleuth's personal growth and transformation over the course of the story. This could involve overcoming obstacles, confronting fears or insecurities, or learning valuable life lessons that shape their character arc and inform their approach to solving the mystery.

5. Secondary Mystery:

Introduce a secondary mystery or series of subplots that intersect with the central investigation, providing additional challenges and obstacles for the sleuth to overcome.

Beat 9: Theories Formed

As the investigation progresses, the sleuth begins to form theories about the murder and potential suspects. Clues are analyzed, alibis scrutinized, and motives explored as the puzzle starts to take shape.

1. Initial Speculation:

As the sleuth gathers clues and interviews suspects, they begin to form initial theories about the murder. These theories are based on the evidence they've collected so far and their understanding of the motives and relationships of the people involved. Describe the sleuth's thought process as they piece together the puzzle, weighing different possibilities and considering various scenarios.

2. Red Herrings and False Leads:

Use this beat to further add suspicion to your red herrings. These could take the form of misleading evidence, unreliable witnesses, or seemingly plausible but ultimately incorrect conclusions drawn by the sleuth.

3. Multiple Suspects, Multiple Theories:

Highlight the presence of multiple suspects, each with their own plausible motive for the murder. Show how the sleuth considers different theories based on the evidence and their interactions with the suspects, exploring various scenarios and piecing together the puzzle from different angles.

4. Motives and Opportunities:

Explore the motives and opportunities of each suspect, examining their alibis and relationships with the victim to assess their likelihood of being the murderer. You can use this beat to further build on the initial motives established in act one.

5. Uncovering Secrets:

As the investigation progresses, the sleuth uncovers secrets and hidden agendas that shed new light on the murder and challenge their existing theories. Show how each new piece of information alters the sleuth's understanding of the case and prompts them to revise their theories accordingly.

6. Process of Elimination:

Use the process of elimination to narrow down the list of suspects and refine the sleuth's theories about the murder. As the investigation unfolds, certain suspects may be ruled out based on their alibis or lack of motive, while others become more suspicious as new evidence comes to light. Show how the sleuth systematically eliminates possibilities and zeroes in on the true culprit, building suspense as the story reaches its climax.

Beat 10: Interviews and Secrets Revealed

The sleuth conducts interviews with suspects and uncovers the secrets they want to keep buried. Each revelation adds a new layer to the mystery, moving the investigation forward.

1. Strategic Interviewing:
Describe the sleuth's approach to conducting interviews with the suspects and witnesses. This could involve careful planning and preparation, including gathering background information on each individual and devising a list of probing questions designed to elicit valuable insights and uncover hidden secrets. Give the sleuth reasons and ways to intersect with the suspects. Make it believable.

2. Questioning Techniques:
Use a combination of empathy, persuasion, and intuition to elicit useful information. This could involve employing open-ended questions to encourage candid responses, probing for inconsistencies or discrepancies in their stories, and paying

close attention to nonverbal cues such as body language and facial expressions that may reveal the truth. During interviews, let the suspects tell one truth and one lie to give the sleuth more food for thought.

3. Revealing Secrets:

Use interviews as a means of revealing secrets and exposing hidden agendas that shed new light on the murder and the motives of the suspects. Show how each revelation adds to the investigation and prompts the sleuth to reassess their theories about the crime.

4. Building Trust:

Illustrate the sleuth's efforts to build trust and rapport with the suspects and witnesses, establishing a comfortable environment that encourages them to open up and share valuable information.

5. Uncovering Clues:

Use interviews as an opportunity to uncover clues and gather evidence that moves the investigation forward. This could involve extracting key information about the suspects' whereabouts, alibis, and relationships with the victim, as well as uncovering physical evidence or corroborating witness testimony that corroborates or contradicts their accounts. Show how each interview brings the sleuth closer to uncovering the truth behind the murder, adding momentum to the investigation and heightening suspense as the story progresses.

6. Revelation of Character:

Use interviews as a means of revealing the true character of the suspects and witnesses, exposing their vulnerabilities, flaws, and moral ambiguities. This could involve exploring their backstory, motivations, and innermost desires, as well as highlighting the complexities of their relationships with the other characters. By delving into the depths of human nature through interviews, you can create richly drawn characters that resonate with readers and add depth to the narrative as the mystery unfolds.

Beat 11: Midpoint, Second Murder

A shocking twist occurs as a second murder (or crime) rocks the community, raising the stakes and complicating the investigation. This midpoint revelation forces the sleuth to reassess their theories and adds urgency to their quest for the truth.

1. Midpoint Twist:

At the midpoint of the story, introduce a twist that upends the sleuth's investigation and shifts the dynamics of the mystery. This could take the form of a second murder—a shocking and unexpected development that raises the stakes and adds urgency to the sleuth's quest for answers. Use the second murder to propel the story into its second act, infusing the narrative with new obstacles, suspects, and clues that keep readers engaged.

2. Increased Tension:

Heighten tension following the second murder, as the cozy setting is once again rocked by tragedy. Show how the residents react to the news, with fear and paranoia spreading through the community as they grapple with the realization that a killer may be lurking in their midst. Use the increased tension to ratchet up the suspense, creating a sense of urgency that drives the sleuth to redouble their efforts to solve the crimes before more lives are lost.

3. Revised Theories:

The second murder forces the sleuth to reassess their theories about the initial crime and consider new possibilities.

4. Character Reactions: Illustrate how the characters react to the second murder, revealing new facets of their personalities and relationships. Some may be overcome with grief and shock, while others may react with suspicion or defensiveness as they come under scrutiny as potential suspects.

5. Parallel Investigations:

Show how the sleuth juggles the investigation of both murders simultaneously, dividing their attention between two separate but interconnected mysteries. Use parallel investigations to create a sense of urgency and momentum in the narrative, as the sleuth races against time to uncover the truth behind both crimes before the killer strikes again.

Act Three

Beat 12: Antagonist Attack

The antagonist, aware of the sleuth's investigation, takes action to thwart their progress. This could manifest as threats, sabotage, or even direct confrontation, posing a significant obstacle to solving the mystery.

1. Heighten Danger:

The antagonist's attack should significantly escalate the level of danger faced by the sleuth. This could involve a physical assault, a threat to their safety, or an attempt to sabotage their investigation. Make it clear that the antagonist will stop at nothing to protect their secrets and prevent the sleuth from exposing the truth, adding urgency to the sleuth's quest for justice.

2. Showcase Sleuth's Resilience:

Use the attack as an opportunity to showcase the

sleuth's resilience and resourcefulness in the face of danger. Whether they narrowly escape the antagonist's clutches or bravely confront them head-on, highlight the sleuth's determination to see justice served and their unwavering commitment to uncovering the truth, even in the face of trouble.

3. Reveal Antagonist's True Nature:

The attack should provide insight into the antagonist's true nature and motivations. This could involve revealing their ruthlessness, cunning, or capacity for violence, as well as shedding light on the reasons behind their actions.

4. Introduce New Clues:

The aftermath of the attack may yield new clues or evidence that brings the sleuth closer to unraveling the mystery. Whether it's a piece of physical evidence left behind by the antagonist or a revelation, use the attack as a catalyst for advancing the investigation and uncovering key information that moves the story forward.

5. Deepen Conflict:

The attack deepens the conflict between the sleuth and the antagonist, setting the stage for a final confrontation that resolves the central mystery. Use the attack as a turning point that pushes the sleuth to confront the antagonist directly, leading to a climactic showdown that determines the outcome of the story.

Beat 13: Stakes Rise

With the antagonist's interference, the stakes escalate, putting not only the sleuth but also those close to them in danger. Tensions mount as the race to uncover the truth becomes increasingly dire.

1. Increasing Danger:

Gradually escalate the level of danger faced by the sleuth and other characters as they delve deeper into the mystery. This could involve physical threats, such as the discovery of a weapon or the presence of a dangerous suspect, as well as psychological threats, such as intimidation or blackmail.

2. Race Against Time:

Introduce a sense of urgency by establishing a deadline or time limit for solving the mystery. This could be a looming threat, such as an impending storm or a deadline set by the antagonist, that adds pressure to the sleuth's investigation and forces them to act quickly. Use the race against time to create suspense and momentum in the narrative, as the sleuth races against the clock to solve the mystery before it's too late.

3. Compromised Safety:

Put the sleuth and other characters in increasingly terrible situations that compromise their safety.

Show how the characters must rely on their wits and resourcefulness to survive.

4. Reputation at Stake:

As suspicions mount and secrets are revealed, the sleuth may find themselves ostracized or targeted by those who wish to keep the truth hidden. Highlight the risks of going against the status quo and the sacrifices the sleuth must make to stand up for what's right.

5. Collateral Damage:

Show how the consequences of the investigation extend beyond the central mystery, affecting other characters. This could involve collateral damage, such as damaged friendships, shattered trust, or irreparable harm to the community's reputation.

Beat 14: Second Interviews, Suspects Narrow

The sleuth conducts another round of interviews, narrowing down the list of suspects based on their evolving theory. Alibis are scrutinized, motives are re-examined, and the true culprit begins to emerge from the shadows.

1. Refined Focus:

After the initial round of interviews and gathering of evidence, the sleuth's focus narrows as they hone in on key suspects who are most likely to have had a motive and opportunity to commit the crime. The second round of interviews is conducted with these prime suspects in mind, allowing the sleuth to delve deeper into their backgrounds, relationships, and potential involvement in the case.

2. Revisit Alibis:

During the second interviews, the sleuth revisits the alibis provided by the suspects during the initial round of questioning. They scrutinize the details, looking for inconsistencies or discrepancies that may cast doubt on the suspects' claims of innocence. By cross-referencing alibis with new evidence or witness statements, the sleuth can further narrow down the list of viable suspects and zero in on the true culprit.

3. Probe Deeper:

In the second interviews, the sleuth probes deeper into the suspects' motives and relationships with the victim, seeking to uncover ulterior motives that may have played a role in the crime. They ask more pointed questions and press for details that were not explored in the initial interviews, drawing out information that may shed new light on the case.

4. Confrontation:

The second interviews may also involve a degree of confrontation, as the sleuth confronts the suspects with inconsistencies or evidence that implicates them in the crime. This can lead to tense exchanges and emotional confrontations as the suspects react to being placed under suspicion and attempt to defend themselves against the accusations.

5. New Clues Revealed:

The second interviews often provide new clues or revelations that move the investigation forward. By following up on leads and pursuing new lines of inquiry, the sleuth gains valuable insights that bring them closer to uncovering the truth.

Beat 15: Final Theory

Armed with new revelations and insights, the sleuth formulates their final theory about the identity of the killer. Clues fall into place, and the pieces of the puzzle start to fit together, leading towards the climactic confrontation.

1. Culmination of Clues:

The final theory should be a culmination of all the clues and evidence gathered throughout the investigation. Review the key pieces of evidence, witness testimonies, and character motivations that have been uncovered along the way, highlighting how each contributes to the sleuth's understanding of the case.

2. Connecting the Dots:

Show the sleuth connecting the dots between seemingly unconnected clues and events, revealing the underlying patterns and motivations that tie everything together. This could involve revisiting earlier scenes or conversations in a new light, as the sleuth uncovers hidden meanings and connections that were previously overlooked.

3. Eliminating Red Herrings:

As the final theory takes shape, the sleuth should systematically eliminate red herrings and false leads that have diverted their attention from the true culprit, unless this was already handled with the second crime or murder.

4. Uncovering the Motive: The final theory should provide a clear motive for the crime, explaining why the culprit acted as they did and how their actions fit into the larger context of the story.

5. Twists and Turns:

Introduce one final twist or unexpected revelation that adds an extra layer of complexity to the final theory. This could involve a shocking confession from an unexpected source, a last-minute discovery that changes everything the sleuth thought they knew, or a dramatic confrontation with the villain that leads to an unexpected outcome. Secondary villains make for wonderful twists!

Beat 16: Lowest Point

Just when it seems like the sleuth is closing in on the killer, they hit a low point. Perhaps a critical piece of evidence is lost, an ally betrays them, or the antagonist gains the upper hand, plunging the protagonist into despair.

1. Revelation of False Leads:

The sleuth discovers that they have been following false leads or misinterpreting evidence, leading them to doubt their investigative skills and the validity of their theories. This revelation shakes the sleuth's confidence and forces them to reassess their approach to the case, leaving them feeling lost and uncertain about how to proceed.

2. Personal Setbacks:

The lowest point may involve personal setbacks or challenges for the sleuth that affect their ability to focus on the investigation.

3. Dead End:

The sleuth hits a dead end in the investigation, unable to uncover any new leads or make progress towards solving the mystery. Despite their best efforts, they come up empty-handed and begin to question whether they will ever be able to solve the case.

4. Betrayal:

The sleuth experiences betrayal from someone they trusted. This could involve a close friend or ally withholding crucial information, double-crossing the sleuth for their own gain, or revealing themselves to be working for the villain all along. Show how this betrayal shakes the sleuth's faith in themselves and those around them, leaving them feeling isolated and vulnerable.

5. Physical Danger:

The sleuth finds themselves in grave physical danger, facing off against the antagonist or another dangerous suspect who will stop at nothing to silence them. Show how the sleuth's bravery is put to the ultimate test as they confront the dangers.

6. Loss of Hope:

The lowest point is marked by a loss of hope for the sleuth, who begins to doubt whether they will ever be able to solve the mystery and bring the villain to justice.

Act Four

Beat 17: Rise from the Ashes

Despite the setback, the sleuth finds the strength to rise from the ashes, determined to see the investigation through to its conclusion. They rally their allies, recommit to their mission, and prepare for the final showdown.

1. Clarity Amidst Chaos:

After reaching their lowest point, the sleuth experiences a moment of clarity where they gain new insights or perspective on the case. This could involve a sudden realization about a piece of evidence, a breakthrough in understanding the villain's motives, or a revelation about their own strengths and abilities as an investigator.

2. Reassurance from Allies:

The sleuth receives support from their allies and sidekicks. This could involve words of encouragement, practical assistance in following up on leads, or a reminder of the sleuth's past successes and resilience in the face of adversity. By drawing strength from their friends and allies, the sleuth regains confidence in themselves and their ability to overcome challenges.

3. New Leads Surface:

Just when all seems lost, new leads or pieces of evidence surface that breathe new life into the investigation.

4. Personal Growth:

The sleuth undergoes personal growth and development as a result of their struggles and setbacks.

This could involve overcoming self-doubt, learning from past mistakes, or finding inner strength in the face of adversity.

5. Adversity Fuels Determination:

Adversity fuels the sleuth's determination to solve the mystery and bring the culprit to justice. Rather than being defeated by their setbacks, the sleuth is spurred on by the challenges they face, determined to prove themselves and overcome the odds stacked against them.

6. Final Push Towards Resolution:

The "rise from the ashes" moment propels the sleuth towards the final resolution of the mystery. With newfound determination and clarity, the sleuth presses forward with renewed energy and purpose, closing in on the truth with each new discovery.

Beat 18: New Plan

With renewed determination, the sleuth devises a new plan to corner the villain and bring them to justice. They strategize, gather their resources, and set the stage for the climactic confrontation.

1. Change in Tactics:

The sleuth adopts a new set of tactics or strategies for gathering information and following up on leads. This could involve going undercover to gather information discreetly, enlisting the help of a trusted ally to gather intelligence, or employing unconventional methods to extract information from reluctant witnesses. By changing their approach, the sleuth hopes to shake things up and break through any barriers that may be hindering their progress.

2. Collaboration with Allies:

The sleuth reaches out to their allies for assistance and support, pooling their resources and expertise to tackle the mystery as a team. By working together, the sleuth and their allies hope to cover more ground and uncover new leads that will bring them closer to stopping the villain and solving the case.

3. Focus on Motive:

The sleuth shifts their focus to the motive behind the crime. By understanding the motive behind the crime, the sleuth hopes to confront the villain and bring them to justice.

4. Utilization of Resources:

The sleuth makes use of all available resources at their disposal, including technology, forensic analysis, and expert advice. This could involve consulting with specialists in relevant fields, such as forensic science or psychology, to gain additional insights into the case.

Beat 19: Killer Revealed, Final Confrontation

In a dramatic climax, the killer's identity is finally revealed, often in a tense confrontation with the sleuth. Motives are laid bare, secrets exposed, and justice is served as the truth is brought to light.

1. Revelation of the Villain:

The sleuth unveils the identity of the antagonist, laying out the evidence and clues that led them to this conclusion. This revelation is often a moment of shock and surprise for the other characters and readers alike, as the true extent of the culprit's deception is brought to light. Show how the sleuth connects the dots and pieces together the puzzle, explaining how each piece of evidence points to the villain's guilt and motive.

2. Motive Exposed:

Along with revealing the villain's identity, the sleuth exposes their motive for committing the crime. This could involve a dramatic confession from the antagonist, a revelation of their past history or personal vendettas, or a deduction based on their actions and behavior throughout the story. Show how the revelation of truth brings resolution to the story, tying up loose ends and providing a sense of closure for the characters and reader alike.

3. Confrontation:

The sleuth confronts the villain in a dramatic showdown where justice will finally be served. This confrontation is often filled with tension and bravery, as the sleuth faces off against the villain. Show how the stakes are at their highest during this moment, as the sleuth must use all their wits and courage to outsmart the antagonist and bring them to justice.

4. Character Growth:

The final confrontation allows for further character growth and development, as the sleuth and other characters reflect on their experiences and the lessons learned throughout the investigation. This could involve a moment of self-realization for the sleuth, as they come to terms with their own strengths and weaknesses as an investigator, or a moment of redemption for other characters who may have played a role in the mystery. By showing how the characters evolve and grow as a result of their experiences, you create a satisfying conclusion to the story.

Beat 20: Resolution

With the mystery solved and the killer apprehended, order is restored. Loose ends are tied up, relationships are reconciled, and the community can once again return to its tranquil existence, albeit with a newfound awareness of the darkness that lurks beneath the surface.

1. Culprit Apprehended:

The resolution typically involves the culprit being apprehended and brought to justice. This could involve their arrest by the authorities, a confession of guilt, or some other form of accountability for their actions.

2. Character Arcs:

The resolution is an opportunity to explore the character arcs of the sleuth and other key characters. Reflect on how they've evolved throughout the story, what they've learned from their experiences, and how they've grown as individuals.

3. Community Impact:

Consider how the resolution of the mystery affects the community in which it takes place. Does it bring closure for the residents, or does it leave lingering questions and tensions?

4. Final Revelations:

In some cases, the resolution may involve final revelations or twists that provide additional closure for readers. This could involve tying up loose ends related to subplots or secondary characters, resolving unanswered questions, or delivering a final surprise that leaves readers satisfied.

5. Sense of Closure:

Ultimately, the resolution should provide a sense of closure for readers, tying up all the major plot threads and leaving them feeling satisfied with the outcome.

Beat 21: Equilibrium Restored

Restoring equilibrium is the final step after the resolution, where the sleuth returns to a state of normalcy. This phase wraps up any remaining loose ends. The final image of our sleuth in their world should leave the reader pleased with the way the story finished and eager to re-read the book to find clues they may have missed. Or to read into the next book of the series.

1. Rebuilding Trust:

In the aftermath of the mystery's resolution, characters within the town may need to rebuild trust and repair relationships that were strained during the investigation. This could involve apologies, forgiveness, and acts of reconciliation as they come to terms with the events that unfolded and move forward together.

2. Return to Routine:

With the mystery solved, and the villain apprehended, life in the town returns to its usual rhythm.

Characters resume their daily routines and activities, whether it's running their businesses, tending to their hobbies, or enjoying leisurely pastimes with friends and neighbors.

3. Celebration and Reflection:

The town may come together to celebrate the resolution of the mystery and reflect on the events that unfolded. Alternatively, the sleuth can do so on their own or with close friends and family.

4. Looking to the Future:

As equilibrium is restored, the sleuth looks to the future with optimism and hope. This could involve making plans for the days ahead, setting new goals, or simply embracing the opportunities that lie ahead (such as a date they've been putting off with a romantic interest.) Show how the resolution of the mystery marks a new beginning for the sleuth, opening doors to new possibilities.

5. Closing Thoughts (optional):

Consider including closing thoughts or reflections from the sleuth or another key character, offering a final perspective on the events of the mystery and what they've learned from the experience. This provides readers with a sense of closure and reinforces the themes and messages of the story.

COZY MYSTERY CRIME BRAINSTORM

1. Description of victim and crime:
See Victim and Suspects for more details.

- Victim:
- Name:
- Age:
- Occupation:
- Relationship to Suspect:
- Any distinguishing characteristics or secrets:

2. Murder Location and Time:

- Where does the murder take place?
- What time of day or night does it occur?
- How does the location contribute to the mystery (e.g., isolated, public place)?

3. Suspects:

See Victim and Suspects for more details.

(Use the Author Murder Board to help visualize your suspects better.)

- List potential suspects and their relationship to the victim.
- What motives might each suspect have for wanting the victim dead?
- Are there any alibis or suspicious behaviors that could implicate them?

4. Murder Motive:

See Antagonist Development Template for more details.

- What drives the murderer to commit the crime?
- Explore possible motives such as jealousy, revenge, greed, or blackmail.
- How does the motive tie into the victim's backstory or conflicts with suspects?

5. Method of Murder:

See Antagonist Development Template for more details.

- How is the murder carried out?

- Consider various methods such as poisoning, strangulation, drowning, or staged accidents.
- How does the chosen method reflect the personality or resources of the murderer?

6. Murder Weapon or Means:
See Antagonist Development Template for more details.

- What object or tool is used to commit the murder?
- How does the murderer obtain or access the weapon?
- Is the murder weapon something common or unexpected and does it leave any clues behind?

7. Cover-Up or Red Herrings:
See Antagonist Development Template for more details.

- How does the murderer attempt to cover their tracks or mislead investigators?
- What false leads or red herrings are planted to divert suspicion from the real culprit?
- Are there any unexpected twists or

complications that arise during the investigation?

8. Clues and Evidence:

- Identify key clues or pieces of evidence that lead the protagonist closer to solving the murder.
- How are these clues discovered, and what do they reveal about the identity of the murderer?
- Consider how the clues might be interpreted differently by suspects and investigators.

AUTHOR MURDER BOARD

Use this murder board table style plotter to figure out the spiderweb of your suspect relations. This board is set up in a similar fashion to the classic game of Clue. You know the one I mean... It was the butler in the library with a candlestick! The thing about this game is it is based on traditional mystery solving techniques, which are perfect for our purposes as writers.

First thing is to fill out the names of the suspects. From here, you will go through and add each suspect's motive to the table. After that we can fill in their relationship to the victim and start going through each suspect to note their relationship to one another. Keep in mind, not all suspects will know each other at all or have direct connection and that is just fine! It's alright to keep some of the table blank. Whatever makes sense to your mystery and story.

And there you have it! A perfect spiderweb of suspect connections, or, as I like to call, your Author Murder Board.

Author Murder Board

SUSPECT	1:	2:	3:	4:
MOTIVE				
RELATION TO VICTIM				
RELATION TO SUSPECT 1	✗			
RELATION TO SUSPECT 2		✗		
RELATION TO SUSPECT 3			✗	
RELATION TO SUSPECT 4				✗

PART 4
TENSION AND PACING

MASTERING THE ART OF PACING

Pacing is important in any novel. It is what defines the flow of your novel and determines your reader's interaction with the plot. It becomes that much more dire to get the pacing right in a mystery book since building up tension as your sleuth races to solve a crime can make or break how your reader feels about the book. With that in mind, I always encourage writers to concentrate on the pacing of their cozy mystery the same way they did all the other elements prior to beginning to write.

In the last section, we went through the plotting of the book, which to me is the biggest task you have ahead of you. Hopefully, after reading the section and making your way through the provided resources and templates, you are well on your way to having the plot of your mystery in place. Pat yourself on the back, dear writer, because the hard part is done.

It seems like this might be the perfect time to take a step back and switch gears. Let's talk about pacing and see how we can perfect it in your current plot.

To start, we must understand what pacing is in

order to write it well. Pacing is the speed with which your story is told. Back in the days of verbal storytelling, people used their voice to control the pacing of the story. Descriptions were told in slow, poetic phrases. Action scenes were portrayed with fast loud words and a lot of physical motions to match. Secrets were whispered in hushed tones to the audience. The same rules apply to the written word, but instead of using our vocal cords, we rely on paragraphs and sentences to do the heavy lifting.

There are many ways to control the pace of a book but for cozy mysteries, I think it's important to concentrate on balancing action and introspection, building up the suspense as the story moves along, and working out a chapter structure that keeps the readers turning the pages late into the night. One more chapter cannot apply enough in this case!

We will go over those three elements in more detail in this section, so make sure you have a notebook nearby to take notes. For now, I'd like to offer you some other quick tips on how to control the pacing in your novel, starting with the plot.

The fastest way to test the pacing of your novel is to look at the beats you are hitting in your story. This is where we go back to our plotting sheets and dissect them further. I find it helps to take each beat and write them out on a card or post-it note, then arrange them in the order they follow. Now you can step back and read the notes to see if the pacing builds up to the final moment of catching the villain. The pace of your book should follow upward momentum, settling at the top for a final resolution. Unlike the amateur sleuth's story arc, the overall arc of your cozy mystery will continue to get faster and more dire as the pacing increases.

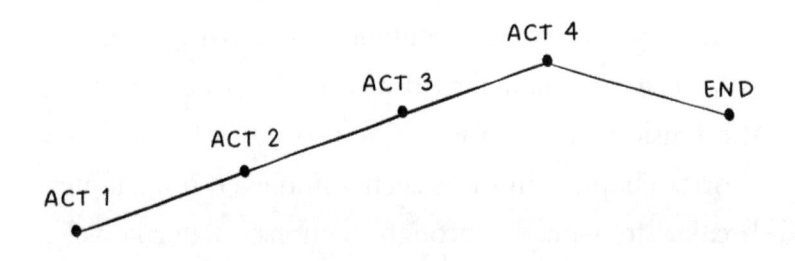

```
                          ACT 4
                           •
                  ACT 3  /   \
                   •    /     \   END
           ACT 2  /            \  •
            •   /
   ACT 1  /
    •
```

As you're studying your beats, if you find that any of them lag or dragging down that arc, it needs to be either repositioned to earlier in the story or made to have a faster pace. There are several ways to do this and one way I like to employ is to add the discovery of clues. Nothing gets the heart pumping more than another clue to help solve the mystery. We will cover more about building up tension in your pacing in a later chapter, but keep clues in mind when thinking of how to speed up the pacing of a slower plot.

Another plot tip is to watch out for a saggy middle. Stories naturally tend to slow down in the second and third act as we begin to go through multiple interviews on a loop. Adding faster scenes such as chases, threats to the sleuth, clues (mentioned above), and subplots helps keep up the pace to avoid the reader getting bored with repetitive tasks.

When finding yourself stuck in a rut with the pacing of your story, try playing with different sentence lengths, alternating words, and working on paragraph structure. If you're writing a chase or fight scene, stick to shorter sentences and paragraphs. It will make the reader read at a faster pace and raise the tension in the story. It is also advisable to have shorter chapters in these scenes and even use chapter breaks to speed through actions. Alternatively, moments of introspection could use longer, prose-like sentences, fuller paragraphs, and chapters that take the time to describe everything in your sleuth's surroundings in great detail.

See what the occasion calls for and tailor your writing accordingly.

Finally, and I'm sure you've heard this a million times before, show and don't tell. Use all the senses when you're writing to control the pacing of your book. Instead of summarizing what tour sleuth is doing, put the reader in their head. What do they see? What do they hear? What do they smell? What can they feel on their fingertips? Let the reader in on what your sleuth's body is going through in order to connect them to the inner pace of your mystery. For example, if your sleuth is about to confront the villain, chances are the pacing will be fast as we are getting ready for the final confrontation. The sleuth's heart will probably be beating against their rib cage, their back might be rigid and tight, they might reach a trembling hand for a flashlight and it will slip out of their slick-covered hands. Immerse your reader in the action in order to work them into the pacing of the story.

It can be difficult to know how to balance action with slower moments of research and thought, especially in a cozy mystery where searching for clues happens constantly. What do you say we discuss how you can achieve this balance without ripping your hair out? Let's go!

CHAPTER 11

Balancing Action and Introspection

The most intriguing part of a cozy mystery book is being able to get to know the sleuth and other characters while simultaneously solving a complicated crime. On paper, the task of writing such a book seems easy enough, but the truth is, doing this right depends on a delicate balance. It is our job as writers to make certain the reader is getting the correct amount of action and introspection in order for the mystery to truly click.

We'll get into the details of how to successfully do both shortly, but for now, I'd like to quickly comment on what I mean by each.

Action, or in this case the meat of solving the crime, can be anything from physical assertion scenes to those that require more of a mental effort. The action in a cozy mystery is often heavily skewed towards the detecting portion of the sleuth's journey. Things like searching for clues, solving puzzles, and confronting the suspects, and finally the villain, all fit under the action umbrella.

Introspection, on the other hand, are the slower more description-based scenes. Your introspection could focus on the sleuth's inner monologues as they solve the crime, the dialog they have with other characters, and the general description of place in your world. It is easy to tell introspection from action based on sentence structure and pacing, something we recently discussed.

In order to achieve the balance I mentioned above, there are a few tricks and tips you can use to help you along.

Establishing the Pace

- Begin by establishing a rhythm that alternates between moments of action and introspection. Starting on an action scene in your first chapter sets the pace for the rest of the book, so make sure you can keep up with this promise if that is the way you choose to go.
- Use action sequences to propel the plot forward, introducing clues, suspects, and red herrings.

- When working with action scenes, make sure you are alternating between the types of action scenes you are using. Too many interviews in a row will slow down the pace, while too many clues and puzzles can drive a reader mad. Switch between these as you write to always keep the forward momentum going.
- Follow up intense action scenes with quieter, introspective moments to allow characters—and readers—to process new information and emotions. The slow scenes in your novel can be added throughout to avoid lag.

Character Development through Introspection

- Use introspection to unearth your protagonist's thoughts, feelings, and motivations. Be careful not to do this too often because an amateur sleuth should be proactive and not live in their head. With that said, we all have thoughts that refuse to leave us alone and a reader will expect that level of realism. A good way to check for too much inner monologue is

to take a look at the length of your paragraphs. If you find you have too many long paragraphs in a row, try to cut them down by inserting short bursts of action.
- Your sleuth's motivations can also be a good way to add introspection. Make them reflect on their goals once in a while or hint at them via dialog with the supporting cast.
- Allow readers to connect with the protagonist on a deeper level by uncovering their fears, doubts, and personal growth. We covered this in more detail in the character development section, but I wanted to add it again since it relates to the introspection of the plot as well.
- Intersperse introspective moments with action to maintain momentum while providing insight into the protagonist's inner world. A rule of thumb I have is every thought or description should be either proceeded or followed by an action. For example, if my sleuth has long moments of pondering a theory, I will

usually inject a clue in the midst of it to pick up the pace. It helps even more when that clue negates the theory and gives the sleuth a roadblock to overcome.

Balancing Dialog and Inner Monologue

- Utilize dialog to drive the plot forward and reveal information through interactions between characters. Your interviews will do a big bulk of the heavy lifting here, but do include many moments of the sleuth interacting with the supporting cast. No one is an island and our sleuth is no exception. I find in cozy mysteries, relying on other characters for help not only forms a sense of community but gives me a chance to world build and develop the sleuth without info dumping.
- Pair dialog with inner monologue to provide readers with insight into the sleuth's thoughts and suspicions. This works especially well if you have alternate POVs, a tool I sometimes employ in my books. In Orchard Hollow, there are

chapters added from several POVs helping drive the story. I even have Harry Houdini, the raccoon, narrating one!
- Strike a balance between dialog-heavy scenes and moments of introspection to keep the narrative flowing smoothly.

Incorporating Setting

- Use setting descriptions to evoke mood and atmosphere, enhancing both action and introspective moments. As you sleuth physically moves through the world, don't forget to describe their surroundings. Use all the senses when doing so to show and not tell.
- Use setting changes to signal shifts in pacing. A new location and its description can do a lot for the pace of the novel and to help strike a balance between action and introspection. For example, if your sleuth is knee-deep in research, put them in a library and describe the setting. It would be quiet, possibly in dim lighting, if the text is antiquated and protected. Describe the smell of old books, the sound of pages flipping filling the air, the

way the librarian's glasses perch on the tip of her nose. Then throw your sleuth out into the world in the next chapter and have them move at a faster clip. The changes in location will drastically improve the balance set in your book.

Resolving Conflict

- Use introspective moments to tie up loose ends and reveal the hidden truths behind the mystery. This is especially useful as your sleuth formulates theories and brings the mystery to a close.

The balance between action and introspection is a thin line us writers must walk. When I am finished with the first draft of my books, I tend to backtrack and make notes on the action and introspection scenes in the story. Color-coding is a great tool to use here since you can get a good bird's-eye view of where you might be heavy in one over the other. Always remember that editing is your best friend when it comes to writing cozy mysteries and you will have a chance to strike the balance we discussed in this chapter, even if you don't do so when drafting.

As you learn how to develop and create balance

in your story, you will naturally be on your way to the next part of successful whodunits. I think you're ready to start thinking about suspense and tension, and how to build them up in your book to make the reader squirm!

CHAPTER 12

Building Up Suspense

The tension in a mystery book is the glue that holds it together. So far, we have developed characters that our readers will root for, analyzed and created their world, and plotted out the story. But what about the suspense that readers expect from a cozy mystery?

In the cozy genre, the suspense of a story plays as much of a role as it would in any other narrative where discovery is involved. We want the reader's heart pounding as they race against time with your sleuth to solve the crime. To get this reaction, and other physical and emotional responses, we have to build up the suspense until the final confrontation.

We do this by using tension. If you've done your job right, your cozy mystery will start with very little tension and slowly increase until it is ready to snap. Think of the suspense in your book as a string that you are stretching from one end of the story to the next; at some point, the length of the string will run out. That end point is exactly where we want to be.

But how do we get there?

The beats I have provided naturally build up the suspense in your novel, so if you followed that template, you are already well on your way. Additionally, you can use the following tips to add more dimension to the suspense of your book and really make that string stretch out.

Withholding Information

Give readers just enough information to pique their curiosity, but not enough to solve the mystery right away. Introduce clues gradually, keeping some key details hidden until the right moment.

Actionable tips:

- Introduce your mystery gradually, revealing just enough to hook readers but leaving key details obscured. You want the story to have a drip effect where you reveal information little by little. This could come in the form of lead up to a body or even dual timelines.

- Use misdirection to keep readers guessing, leading them down one path while the true solution remains hidden. This is where your red herrings will come into play heavily.

Atmosphere and Setting

Use the setting to enhance the mood and atmosphere of your story. A dark, eerie setting can create a sense of foreboding, while a bustling city can add urgency and tension.

Actionable tips:

- Tailor the setting to match the tone of your story; for example, a remote, isolated location can enhance feelings of suspense and isolation.
- Use the setting to mirror the internal struggles of your characters, reinforcing the mood and themes of your narrative. Try to use darker, more atmospheric settings in acts two and three as your sleuth is beginning to unravel the mystery and their anxiety with solving the crime sets in.

Foreshadowing

Drop subtle hints and clues early on that will pay off later in the story. This can create anticipation and keep readers engaged as they try to piece together the mystery.

Actionable tips:

- Be strategic in your placement of foreshadowing elements, ensuring they blend seamlessly into the narrative without feeling forced.
- Provide enough clues for attentive readers to pick up on, but also maintain an element of mystery to keep them engaged. I think of these as Easter Eggs and sometimes go as far as to add them to the covers of my books.

Unreliable Narrator

Use a narrator or point-of-view character who may not be entirely trustworthy. This adds an extra layer of uncertainty and keeps readers questioning the validity of the information they're given. You can use the lack of knowledge your sleuth has to do this successfully. The more they find out, the more the reader will begin to question the mystery being solved and everything that they have discovered.

Actionable tip:

- Drop subtle inconsistencies or contradictions in the narrator's account to sow seeds of doubt in the reader's mind. This will work especially well if your sleuth is on the line to be implicated in the crime.

Twists and Turns

Incorporate unexpected plot twists and revelations to keep readers on their toes. Surprise endings or sudden revelations can heighten the suspense and make the resolution more satisfying.

Actionable tips:

- Establish expectations early on, then flip them on their head with unexpected plot twists and revelations.
- Introduce new information or

perspectives that fundamentally change the reader's understanding of the story.
- Make sure that plot twists are supported by the groundwork you have laid earlier in the plot and avoid last-minute surprises that feel contrived.

One of the best advice I had received when I started to write mystery was that to build the tension, I had to put roadblocks in my protagonist's way until they hit rock bottom. I use that advice to this day and it has never steered me wrong. If you think your sleuth has it too easy, chances are, the reader agrees. Make it difficult for them to solve the crime. We are already asking our readers to hold on to their disbelief about an amateur sleuth investigating crimes the police can't solve; adding suspense and tension to the story can help level that disbelief out.

There is one more tip I have for adding suspense to your cozy mystery, but I'd like to talk about it in more detail, which is why it gets its own chapter. Speaking of chapters, let's discuss how you can use chapter structure to build up the tension in your mystery. Ready?

CHAPTER 13

Chapter Structure and Cliffhangers

The way you lay out your chapters and scenes will have a massive effect on not only pacing and suspense, but the overall thematic mood of your cozy mystery. Long chapters full of prose take the reader on a visceral journey of discovery. Short, fast-clipped chapters make their heart race in their chest. Even the placement of integral chapter moments plays a part in how a reader perceives the book. With that in mind, it becomes apparent that chapter structure in a cozy mystery has a significant effect on the mystery as a whole.

Chapter structures will change from book to book and from author to author, but there are a few qualifying factors that we cannot avoid. For our purposes here, I'd like to touch on a few pieces of chapters structure that I employ in my cozy mysteries that help me hook readers and keep those pages turning.

But first, let's touch on what the chapter structure is for in a cozy mystery book.

Understanding Chapter Structure

The cozy mystery chapter, or any chapter in a fiction book, will have a few similar points (or beats) that you should try to hit as a writer.

Opening:

- The setup to what is to come. Hook the reader immediately by starting on the action. Action does not have to be physical, but it's important for the plot to move at a faster pace at the start.
- Show what the goals are either for your sleuth or for the overall mystery.
- Hint at a conflict coming up.

Setting:

- Establish the timeline. You want your reader to know where and when they are so they can concentrate on the story and not on the guesswork of what is happening.
- Add mood and atmosphere by incorporating setting descriptions in each chapter. Cozy mystery readers love a good setting, so use this to your advantage.

- Show don't tell. Use all the senses.

Conflict:

- Think about your sleuth's goals and put obstacles in their way of reaching them.
- The conflict in each chapter doesn't have to be large scale. In A Grave Roast, my initial chapter conflict was a broken espresso machine, preventing Piper from succeeding in her cafe. This conflict wasn't life or death, but it was a dire situation for my sleuth. Consider all levels of obstruction when adding conflict to the chapter: physical and emotional.

Ending:

- Use a satisfying resolution but add foreshadowing to drive the mystery forward.
- Add a lead up to the next chapter to come.

Crafting Compelling Cliffhangers

Speaking of lead up, cliffhangers are a wonderful way of making certain your reader wants to turn the page and move to the next chapter. I use these all the time in my own writing as a way of driving the plot and adding compulsion to the reader experience.

There are a few ways to treat cliffhangers to get the most out of them:

- Increase tension throughout the chapter, heightening suspense with each passing paragraph. Use the tips for sentence structure to do this well.
- Strategically position cliffhangers at the end of chapters to propel readers forward, leaving them eager to uncover the next twist in the plot.
- One of the best ways to end a chapter is to leave key questions unanswered at the chapter's close, sparking curiosity and driving readers to continue reading.
- In a cozy mystery, your sleuth will be put in impossible situations, some even life threatening. End chapters with characters facing difficult decisions or unexpected

revelations, intensifying emotional investment and suspense.

Common Pitfalls to Avoid

Structuring your chapters in an addictive manner can be a really fun exercise. However, as with most things in writing and any creative craft, there are some mistakes we all make when drafting. Some of the more common ones I have seen and have fallen prey to myself are:

- Overuse of Cliffhangers: Be mindful not to rely too heavily on cliffhangers, as this can diminish their impact and leave readers feeling manipulated. This is especially true for the end of your book—you should never leave a cozy mystery unfinished.
- Lack of Resolution: While cliffhangers are effective for building suspense, ensure that each chapter also provides some resolution or advancement in the plot to satisfy reader expectations. A good rule of thumb is to always answer a question for the reader before asking another one. For example, your sleuth may find a clue in a

chapter that tells them the time and place of the crime, but as they study it further, they realize that the original suspect no longer fits. This forces the reader to ask themselves who the villain might be once more.
- Inconsistent Pacing: Maintain a consistent pace throughout the chapter, balancing moments of tension with quieter, reflective scenes to keep readers engaged without overwhelming them. We have already discussed pacing for your novel as a whole and this is also true at the chapter level.

The way you lay out your chapter will help you create consistency and unity in the book and within the layers of the mystery. The best advice I can give you is to work on the first three chapters and figure out the structure of those first before moving on to the rest of the book. The first three chapters of a cozy mystery give us enough of the beats (see plot section) to help set up the structure of the chapters to come. Once you have those perfected, you can draft as messily as you'd like for the rest of the story.

I can guarantee that if you get the structure of

your chapters right, your readers will be salivating to read not only this book but all the ones to come.

Now that we have the nuts and bolts of the cozy mystery established, we can talk about the writing portion of the novel experience. The cozy mystery writer has the ability to play with several writing styles and your author voice will naturally come out, but there are always connecting tissues that keep readers attached to the genre. That is what we will be concentrating on in the following section.

PART 5
WRITING STYLE

WRITING STYLE AND TONE

When it comes to crafting a bestselling whodunit, atmosphere, and mood are king in cozy mysteries. Readers expect to be immersed in worlds that are both familiar and strange, comforting and tense. All in all, we constantly want to push and pull our readers as we take through the plot, and the best way to do that is with our writing style.

The language used in cozy mysteries is often light, witty, and accessible, with a focus on clever wordplay and humor. Our job, dear writer, is to employ descriptive language to evoke a sense of coziness and nostalgia, transporting readers to a world they wouldn't want to leave. That is not to say that you need to overdo it with prose and frills that might not earn your reader's attention. You should always stay true to your own author voice, as that will be the thing that unites your books and defines your writing career.

My own author voice is very direct, with little emphasis on unnecessary details. I enjoy writing fast action and when I focus on description, I often use them as a means of building character or world, not for any other reason. This was not always the case. Throughout my writing career, I have experimented heavily in different writing styles until I found one that fits. I still continue to experiment to this day by trying out genres that are new to me, especially in short story form.

As you're looking for your own author voice, I encourage you to do the same. Write shorter fiction in different styles of voice until you find one that resonates best with you.

Similarly, the tone of your cozy mystery will vary depending on the plot, the mystery, and the sub-genre of cozy you're writing. Paranormal cozies, for example, are often heavily imbued with humor, making their tone lighter. This is done intentionally to prevent the genre from leaning too heavily into fantasy and losing its grip on the cozy mystery the reader expects.

In this section, we are going to cover reader expectations when it comes to the craft of writing a cozy mystery. We will discuss the tone of the genre in more detail, touch on POV and how to use your chosen one to your benefit, and talk about injecting humor into your cozy to make it stand out. This section is dedicated to the technical part of writing, which I strongly believe is one of the more dominant aspects of a cozy mystery that makes readers pick up books.

Not sure about you but I am ready to talk writing style!

CHAPTER 14

Cozy Mystery Writing Style

Cozy mysteries stand apart from other mysteries and thrillers because of their very distinct writing style. In a cozy, emphasis is often placed on the details since those are the things that will make the reader attached to the story. The statement **the Devil is in the details** has never applied more than it does to writing cozy mysteries.

If this is your first time writing in the genre, I highly recommend you start to bulk up your TBR with cozy mystery books. Read them from the perspective of an author and make notes on the type of language used, the point of view chosen, and the tone depicted in the words and descriptions. All of these are good indications of genre expectation and what you should strive for in your own writing.

Let's take a deeper look at each one so we can better understand their place.

Language

Use descriptive language to paint a vivid picture of your setting, immersing readers in its sights, sounds, and smells. From the layout of streets to the scent of salt in the air at a seaside resort, every detail contributes to the cozy atmosphere. The more detail you can provide in your passages, the more the reader will feel like they are part of the story. While your story does not need to lean too heavily on prose, do look at your manuscript on a sentence by sentence level and make certain that the language is appealing and draws the reader in. We are aiming for cozy descriptions that make us feel like we are tucked in under a warm blanket with a good book while the rain is rapping against the window. Even the sentence I just wrote could be a good example of atmosphere building.

Dialog plays a crucial role in cozy mysteries, providing insight into characters' personalities, relationships, and motivations. Keep the dialog natural and authentic, reflecting the distinct voices of your characters. Pepper conversations with humor (see next chapter), and subtle clues, but avoid overly formal or stilted language. Dialog should flow seamlessly, engaging readers and propelling the story forward.

A tip for dialog is to make a list of all your main characters, or those who will have speaking roles, and jot down their personality traits. Under each character, make a note of their style of speaking. From here, you can start building a database of sayings each character might have. I've created a sample list for Stella Rutherford, the ghost familiar and supporting character in Orchard Hollow. Take a look and see if you can immediately picture the woman in your head based on this.

STELLA RUTHERFORD

RICH, SNOBBY, CARES A LOT ABOUT APPEARANCES, HAS A SMART ANSWER FOR EVERYTHING. CAN'T SIT WITH US ENERGY

SPEECH STYLE: SLOW AND CALCULATED. NO EYE CONTACT, OFTEN LOOKS AT HER NAILS AND APPEARS BORED.

NOTABLE SAYINGS:
- NOT TO BRAG BUT...
- THAT IS SO LAST SEASON IT PHYSICALLY HURTS ME
- SPEAK FASTER PLEASE, I'M ON MY ONLY AFTERLIFE HERE

Once you're done with your list, you should have a better idea of how everyone will sound in a conversation and you can continue to build on these lists as you write.

Point of View

Intimate Third Person

Cozy mysteries typically employ a third-person point of view, allowing readers to observe the unfolding events through the eyes of the sleuth or an omniscient narrator. This intimate perspective enables readers to connect with the sleuth, empathize with their struggles, and share in their triumphs. Maintain a consistent point of view throughout the narrative to avoid confusion and maintain reader immersion. In order to avoid head-hopping in this style, it helps to focus on one character in each scene or chapter so your reader doesn't get confused on the central subject of the story.

Limited Omniscience

While cozy mysteries often utilize a third-person perspective, at times, they employ limited omniscience, granting readers access to the thoughts and emotions of the sleuth while preserving the mystery surrounding other characters. This selective revelation of information heightens suspense and keeps readers guessing until the final reveal. It is also a great way to add more personality into an otherwise big-picture POV.

Cozy Confidante - First Person

Another effective point of view in cozy mysteries is the first person. By adopting this perspective, the sleuth becomes the reader's focus, dragging them into their world and sharing their thoughts, fears, and observations firsthand. This creates an immediate connection between the reader and the sleuth. The first person POV is becoming more and more common in the genre and is especially common in paranormal cozies.

Tone

The tone of a cozy mystery is typically light-hearted and charming. While the central mystery may be serious, the overall atmosphere should be inviting and comforting. Balance moments of suspense with moments of laughter and lightness, ensuring that readers feel both engaged and uplifted throughout the story.

One thing I like to keep in mind when writing is that my tone will define the style of writing, which will determine the mood of the reader. When I am serious, that tone gets transported to the writing and with such, to the reader.

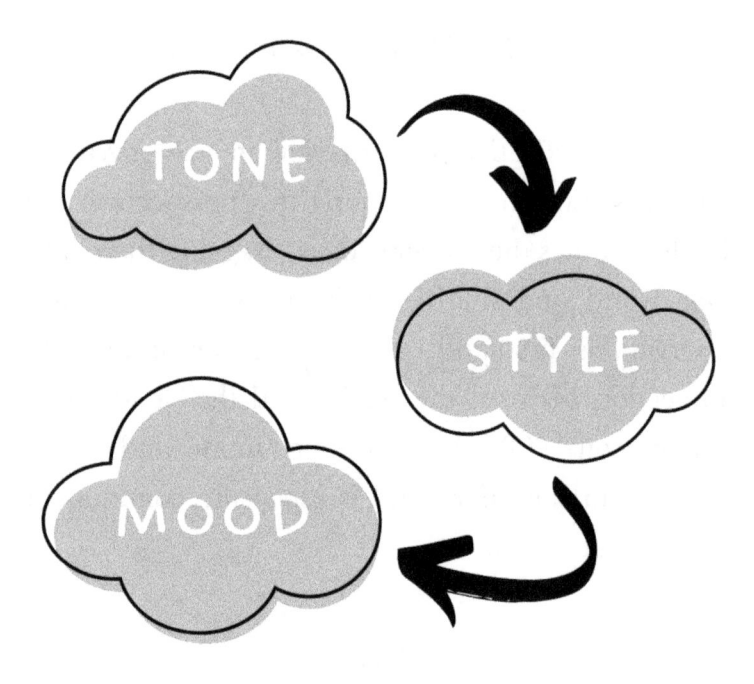

TONE → STYLE → MOOD → (cycle)

By working on your tone as you write, the style of your language will change and it will, in turn, influence how a reader perceives different plot points. If you are someone who enjoys music while you write, I suggest making different playlists for different tones and moods you'd like to portray. Then you can put them on to help set yourself up for success as you work on specific parts of the story.

The style of your writing will change as you continue to work in the genre, so please don't put too much pressure on yourself to get it right the first time. Instead, spend more time developing your author voice, which will be what makes readers continue to pick up your books. In case you're wondering what I mean when I refer to your specific author voice, it is the unique style, tone, and perspective that an author brings to their writing. It's the distinctive way in which an author communicates their ideas, emotions, and narrative to the reader. Just like a person's speaking voice can be recognized by those who know them well, an author's voice can often be recognized by readers familiar with their work. It encompasses aspects such as vocabulary choice, sentence structure, pacing, and the overall mood or atmosphere of their writing.

Most importantly, and as I mentioned earlier on, read, my dear writer. Read as much as your little heart desires to help inspiration flow.

Injecting Humor into the Cozy Mystery

When in doubt, add humor to your cozy mystery. It is a sure way to make people feel at home and relaxed as they make their way through the mystery. Speaking of giggles, injecting humor into your book can make it stand out from the rest, especially when the jokes land. I use a lot of humor in Orchard Hollow in order to make the characters more relatable and their relationships be more appealing to my readers.

Ways to add laughs to a novel and to keep the reader engaged are:

1. Character Quirks and Eccentricities

One effective way to inject humor is through your characters' quirks and eccentricities. These idiosyncrasies can provide comedic relief and make your characters more memorable. Consider giving your protagonist and supporting characters unique traits that lend themselves to humorous situations.

Piper, for example, is incredibly clumsy and I use that to my advantage by pitting the world against her. Combining her many accidents with Stella Rutherford's sharp tongue lends moments of banter throughout the narrative that readers react to instantly.

2. Dialog and Banter

With my example in mind, consider using banter between your characters as a way to develop their relationships further. Dialog is a powerful tool for adding humor to your novel. Clever comebacks and humorous exchanges between characters can lighten the tone of your story and entertain your readers. Pay attention to the rhythm and timing of your dialog to maximize comedic effect. Bonus points if you can add physical moments of humor to really drive the banter home.

Experiment with wordplay, sarcasm, and irony to add depth to your conversations.

3. Humorous Narration

The narrator's voice plays a crucial role in setting the tone of your cozy mystery. Experiment with playful language, clever observations, and funny asides to add a layer of entertainment to your narrative.

If you haven't written humorously before, I encourage you to read comedic works, watch stand up comedy, and listen to podcasts that guarantee a giggle. Putting yourself in the mood to laugh is the first step to having that feeling take root in your writing as well.

However you decide to write your mystery, the crucial part to developing your writing style is simply to keep writing. Write every chance you can until you can step back and find a sense of voice in your work. Once you get there, use it to propel you forward. Submerge that voice in your words and watch as your cozy mystery begins to take shape. It might take some time, but after a while, you will see the hidden nuances in the genre and be able to follow them on instinct.

And don't forget, everything can be fixed in editing. Which is where we are going next!

PART 6
POLISHING YOUR MANUSCRIPT

CHAPTER 15

Revision and Editing Techniques

Ah! The dreaded editing stage of a novel. If this isn't your first book, you know exactly what I'm talking about, and if it is, strap in for a wild ride! Editing can be a grueling process for some, myself included, but it is the key to polishing a manuscript to get it is ready to move to the next stages of publishing. Now that you have drafted your novel, it is time to look at it with fresh eyes and begin your rounds of self-editing.

Every author has their own way of editing their words. In this section, I'm going to share with you my stages of editing and you can feel free to use them all or incorporate parts into your current editing process however you see fit. I will be noting these in the exact order I take my books through, so grab a pen and paper and let's get started.

1. Reviewing the Plot

The first thing I do when editing is look at the plot overall. You can begin by revisiting your plot outline or story structure. Check for any plot holes or inconsistencies. Make notes on where additional clues or red herrings might be necessary to keep the reader engaged.

In this phase, I look at the big picture of the story. Usually, this involves reading the full manuscript and making notes on anything that doesn't add up or answering any unanswered questions left behind. After my notes are complete, I go back and revise accordingly.

I should note that while I am writing, I keep an editing notebook nearby (physically or digitally) and it is during this stage that I also make the revisions require I caught while drafting. Because I would like to keep the drafting process fluid, I do not make big picture changes as I write. I do, however, reread what I have written the day before prior to starting another writing session. I find that this helps get me back in the story and allows me to make minor edits as I write to create a polished first draft.

2. Character Development

Once the big picture elements are in place, I move on to the characters. You want to pay close attention to your characters. Do they remain consistent throughout the story? Are their motivations clear and believable? Look for opportunities to deepen character relationships and add layers to their personalities. Cozy mysteries thrive on well-developed characters.

One major alteration I make during the character editing phase is to add more humor to the story. I look at where the pacing of the book is on the slower side and try to inject funny moments or banter in conversation to speed things up and lighten the mood.

3. Pacing and Tension

And since we are discussing pacing, that is the part of story structure I look at next. This time is a great moment to double check all the work you did when plotting the pace and tension in your mystery. Does it build steadily, keeping the reader hooked from start to finish? Add moments of heightened tension where needed.

4. Clues and Red Herrings

In this phase, I backtrack through the clues and see where I can bulk them up. I add small elements and hints into dialog and setting descriptions that give the reader a chance to guess at the final outcome of the mystery.

One thing I rely on heavily here are the senses. I try to use all of them when adding subtle hints. Please note that at times, adding clues may require you to go through the manuscript and rewrite certain parts in order to guarantee the clue does its job and lands well in the mystery.

5. Repeated words

Now this is a big one. For all my books, I have a spreadsheet with repeated words and crutch phrases I tend to use when drafting. That could include anything from single words to full sentences. Whatever gets overused gets added to the document.

Some of my more common overused words are: just, so, glance, grin, heart, as well as connecting sentences with the word "and". I have also included a list of commonly overused words in writing so you can use those as a starting base for your own document.

As I edit, I go down the list and remove or rephrase these words. It is a tedious process, but one that is truly necessary to avoid consistent repetition and poor writing.

6. Alternative phrases

Much as for overused words, I have a running spreadsheet for alternative phrases to use in writing. These are phrases that come to me randomly that I then jot down as I go about my day. The catalog of alternative phrases is constantly growing and I find myself adding to it regularly. I highly recommend that you start this habit if you haven't already.

As I make my way through the manuscript, I cross reference the alternate phrases document to see how I can strengthen sentences and paragraphs with fuller options. For example, instead of "she feared the dark corridor" I will replace the passage with "a shiver tripped down her spine as she stepped into the corridor." That, to me, sounds much more appealing and paints a more vivid picture in the reader's mind.

Alternate phrases are my favorite part of the editing process, and not only because it's the last step of self-editing!

7. Beta Readers and Feedback

When I feel that my manuscript is completed and ready to move to the next step, I enlist the help of beta readers for another set of eyes. My beta readers are a combination of paid and unpaid readers, both of whom I value incredibly as they provide great guidance on the story from a reader perspective.

If you have not yet built your beta reader team, this is your nudge to begin. Your beta readers will give you the type of advice you need to hear before publishing the book and help eliminate poor reviews down the line.

8. Editor pass

Now this editing phase will be different for traditional and self-published authors. Not all self-published authors are able to run their manuscript through a developmental editor due to cost and time restraints, while traditional authors will almost always have one. I have been on the receiving end of both and can definitely say without a doubt that if you can afford to hire a developmental editor as a self-publishing author, do so.

A developmental editor will go through your manuscript and offer advice on how to strengthen plot, character development, the mystery, the setting, and every detail that you may have missed on your own. They have a keen eye for the types of changes that make or break books and, as experienced publishing professionals, I value their insight deeply.

9. Final Copy editing and Proofreading

Before sending your manuscript off to agents or publishers, or publishing it yourself, conduct a thorough proofreading pass. Look for typos, grammatical errors, and formatting issues. I will mention that unless you are in a dire situation, you should always have someone else do these rounds of edits for you. Preferably someone trained in the copy editing and proofreading process.

The last thing any reader wants is to be taken out of the story due to grammatical errors that could have easily been avoided.

Now remember when I said that editing is a grueling process? I hope after this you can see what I meant. With that said, grueling or not, it is crucial to put in the time and properly edit your cozy mystery. We spend so much of ourselves writing the book that it would seem silly to not give it the best chance at success by perfecting it to the best of our abilities.

Guess what, dear writer? With editing out of the

way, we are ready to talk about expansion. That's right! I want to touch base on series writing so you can truly make the most out of your cozy mystery and the world you have created.

COMMONLY OVERUSED WORDS

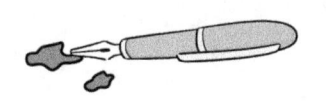

1. Very
2. Really
3. Just
4. Like
5. So
6. Thing
7. Stuff
8. Good
9. Bad
10. Great
11. Amazing
12. Awesome
13. Important
14. Interesting
15. Unique
16. Incredible
17. Excellent
18. Fantastic
19. Wonderful
20. Beautiful
21. Pretty

22. Nice
23. Cool
24. Fun
25. Kind of
26. Sort of
27. Basically
28. Essentially
29. Actually
30. Literally
31. Honestly
32. Truly
33. Clearly
34. Obviously
35. Definitely
36. Seriously
37. Absolutely
38. Honestly
39. Frankly
40. Generally
41. Typically
42. Basically
43. Finally
44. First
45. Secondly
46. Thirdly
47. Firstly
48. Also

49. Additionally
50. Moreover
51. Furthermore
52. However
53. Nevertheless
54. Nonetheless
55. Though
56. Although
57. Even though
58. But
59. Yet
60. Still
61. As
62. Like
63. As if
64. As though
65. As well
66. Likewise
67. Similarly
68. In addition
69. In conclusion
70. On the other hand
71. On the contrary
72. In fact
73. Due to the fact that
74. Because
75. Since

76. Therefore
77. Thus
78. Consequently
79. For example
80. For instance
81. Such as
82. That
83. Which
84. Who
85. Whose
86. When
87. Where
88. Why
89. How
90. What
91. Which
92. Whom
93. Whose
94. A lot
95. Many
96. Some
97. Few
98. Several
99. Most
100. Fewer

PART 7
PLANNING A COZY SERIES

CHAPTER 16

Developing a Series

As you start to read more in the genre of cozy mystery, you might notice a recurring pattern in the books. Most of them are part of a series. The reason for this is that the cozy mystery reader is hungry for new stories, but they are also a very loyal bunch. Once a reader connects with your book and realizes how much they love it, they could go on reading about the shenanigans your sleuth gets into for years to come. I have seen cozy mysteries that span across as many as thirty plus books.

When it comes to cozy mystery series planning, the sky is the limit. I would not recommend you start at thirty books off the top, though. Instead, set your sights on an achievable goal, perhaps five or six books, and go from there. You can always continue to add books or even think about a spinoff in the same world with a different sleuth as the lead.

The reason I give this advice is that you never know where your inspiration might take you. I find after six books I am usually fairly burned out on the world and need to take a break and work on another story to refresh my creative well. You might be in the same boat, so it is always best to err on the side of caution.

Now that you are reaching the end of the book, I'd like to take this final section to talk about the future. If you are interested in series writing, I have a few tips that will help you navigate those turbulent waters and ease you into the process of developing a long-running collection of books.

At the end of this chapter, I have included a cozy mystery series planning notes template as well as a template for the things I track in my series bibles.

Establishing Story Continuity

Character Consistency:
The heart of any cozy series lies in its characters. Ensure that your sleuth maintains core characteristics across all books, while allowing for growth and development. This goes directly back to our character development. If your sleuth has specific ticks or mannerisms, stay on top of them and make certain they don't lose them in the later books.

Setting Details:
Create a vivid and immersive setting that serves

as the backdrop for each mystery. Consistency in locales, landmarks, and atmosphere adds depth to the series. You'd want to make notes on specific locations as you write each book which you can jot down in your series bible for later reference.

Supporting Cast:
Much like your amateur sleuth, the supporting cast also needs to stay consistent throughout the books. Write down what each character looks like and any other notes that relate to them as they step into the story. We don't want to end up having a character come into book four with a different color of eyes or hair that doesn't match their original appearance.

Utilizing Secondary Plots

Character Subplots:
Introduce secondary characters with their own arcs and mysteries woven into the main storyline. These subplots add richness to the narrative and keep readers invested in the series beyond the central mystery. As I mentioned before, I used the secondary plot of Piper's magic in my Orchard Hollow series as the thing that connects the books together. Because of this, the reader has a chance to solve an ongoing mystery throughout all the books and it

keeps the read-through of my books at a higher rate.

Theme Threads:
Use recurring motifs that tie the books together thematically. Whether it's a shared history, a character's backstory, or a town secret, these thematic threads add depth and cohesion to the series.

Sleuth's Character Arc Across the Series

Gradual Evolution:
Plan the sleuth's character arc across the series, allowing them to grow, learn, and confront personal challenges. Each book should contribute to their development, deepening their complexity and enriching their relationships. Do keep in mind that your sleuth's arc will also change from book to book. The arcs in each book should be complete, but you should also try to add growth to your protagonist over the span of the series.

Consistent Core Traits:
While the sleuth may evolve, ensure that their core traits and values remain consistent. This helps readers recognize and connect with the character throughout their adventures in the books. Unlike the physical appearance of the sleuth, their core traits

can slightly alter, they can grow and deepen alongside their arcs. This is especially true for books that feature romance as a subplot, as your sleuth may slowly change overtime when their romantic quests get fulfilled.

Creating a Series Bible

As I mentioned above, there is a series bible template following this chapter in which I included all the things I like to keep track of in my own books. The series bible will become your most prized possession since it will not only help you stay on track with story continuity, but it can help your editors and beta readers too. Use it as a point of reference when you're plotting and writing future books so you never miss a beat. I especially like mine to help me avoid repeating names for side characters or recycling crimes and weapons.

While the series bible provides structure, allow room for flexibility and spontaneity in your storytelling. Embrace new ideas and developments that arise during the writing process, while ensuring they align with the established framework.

Your series bible will become a living organism that will grow with each book. There are many tools you can use to keep your series bible, but my favorite is always in the same place I house my books. If I am using Scrivener to write in my series bible for that project will live in Scrivener. If I am in Dabble, it will live there. You get the point. The purpose of the series bible is to make life easier for you as you write and the best way to accomplish that is to have it be accessible during the drafting process.

Stand-Alone Mysteries with Series Arcs

Balancing Act:
I have already touched on this, but I'd like to reiterate that each book should present a self-contained mystery that can be enjoyed independently. However, interweave overarching series arcs, such as long-standing mysteries or unresolved personal dilemmas, to reward dedicated readers and encourage continued engagement.

Subtle References:
Incorporate subtle references and Easter Eggs to previous books as small hints to all those who are coming back to your world. These nods to past events or characters add a fun touch for past readers without overwhelming new ones.

Organizing the Series Backend

Outline the overarching series arc, including major plot points, character developments, and thematic motifs. This structural framework provides a roadmap for the entire series, ensuring coherence and progression. In the provided series planning template, you will find ideas and questions that can help you begin planning out your series. Don't feel pressured to do it all in one go. You can take your time planning out a series and continue to grow and develop it even as you write the books.

As you organize your series on the backend, I want you to consider how you plan to market it. Think about covers, ads, blurbs, even swag items—anything that will help you get into the spirit of writing the series and keep your eyes on the future.

I absolutely love writing in series format. My longest standing series spans over eight books and one novella, and I have plans in the future for a spinoff in that world. I am also currently working on a spinoff for Orchard Hollow and another cozy mystery book series that might stretch as long as ten books. The beauty of writing in a series is that you never have to leave the world you grow to love. You can continue to revisit your sleuth and the community they belong to as you would an old friend.

To me, there is nothing better than a set of books which feel like home.

SERIES BIBLE TEMPLATE

1. Series Overview:

- Series Title:
- Describe the premise or central theme of your cozy mystery series.
- How many books do you envision for the series?

2. Recurring Characters:

- Protagonist (Amateur Sleuth):
- Name:
- Occupation:
- Quirks/Hobbies:
- Backstory:
- Sidekick or Supporting Characters:
- Names:
- Roles/Relationships to Protagonist:
- Unique Traits or Skills:

3. Setting:

- Describe the town or setting where your cozy mystery series takes place.
- What makes this setting unique or appealing to readers?
- How will the setting evolve or change over the course of the series?

4. Series Arc:

- Outline any overarching story arcs or character development that will unfold throughout the series.
- Are there recurring themes or conflicts that will be explored in each book?
- How will the relationships between characters evolve over time?

5. Themes and Tropes:

- Identify any recurring themes, motifs, or tropes that will be present throughout the series.
- How will you put a unique twist on familiar cozy mystery elements to keep readers engaged?

6. Reader Engagement:

- Consider ways to keep readers invested in your series, such as cliffhangers, foreshadowing, or character development.
- How will you encourage readers to keep coming back for more cozy mysteries?

7. Marketing and Promotion:

- Brainstorm ideas for marketing and promoting your cozy mystery series to attract readers.
- How will you leverage social media, book clubs, and other platforms to build a fan base?

CONCLUSION

Well, my dear writer, you did it! We have come to the end of our adventure in writing a cozy mystery book, and I could not be more proud of you. As we part ways, I want you to think about everything you learned in this book. Let it seep in and take root in your mind. Let it fester. After some time of decompressing, take all those things you learned and use them as your guide to writing your own cozy mystery.

Let's quickly recap everything you learned so you have a summarized road plan to follow.

1. Start with characters. Develop your amateur sleuth first, then follow up with the antagonist and supporting cast. When done, work on your suspects and victims to have a full and engaging cast.
2. World build. Think of the details of your setting and what makes it cozy. Use all the senses and adopt reference images to help

you visualize where your characters will live.
3. It's time to plot! Sit down and think about what is going to happen in your story. Start with breaking down your mystery and puzzle into beats and acts, then work out the details.
4. Go back through your plot and make sure your pacing is intact. Add more tension where needed and supplement with slower-paced scenes to give your sleuth and reader a break from the action.
5. Is your writing style what cozy mystery readers expect? Work on using language that fits the genre and introduce humor to level up your story.
6. With your first draft done, you can begin editing and polishing. Use the editing suggestions I provided to take your manuscript to the next level.
7. Dream big! Use your imagination to come up with more and more books in this amazing world you have created. Build your very own cozy mystery series.

Writing a cozy mystery is, above all else, fun. Never forget that. Much like the tone of your book, a reader can sense when you're loving your own story. With that in mind, I would like to leave you with one last piece of advice. If you ever find yourself in a rut where you don't feel like writing or a story is not coming together, walk away. Leave it alone for a few hours, a few days, a few weeks. Whatever it takes for you to return and love your story again. Never put pressure on yourself to write. Writing is a creative passion and with such, it needs the lightness of your heart and mind to exist on a page. Do not stress, the words will come. And when they do, they will be marvelous!

Well, writer, I think you're ready to start. As we say our goodbyes, know that you have the power to create mysterious worlds and wonderful adventures. Here is to many pages of cozy towns where the mysteries are always brewing, where clues are aplenty, and where readers cannot wait to turn the page for the next chapter. May your imagination never run dry, my friend.

Happy writing!

ABOUT THE AUTHOR

Inessa Sage is a bestselling, award-winning author of mystery and fantasy novels. She has spent most of her life waiting to meet a witch, vampire, or at least get haunted by a ghost. In between failed seances and many questionable outfit choices, she has developed a keen eye for the extra-ordinary.

Inessa spends her free time reading and binge-watching television shows in her pajamas. Currently, she resides in Toronto, Canada with her husband who is not a creature of the night and their daughter who just might be.

She is a Scorpio and a massive advocate of leggings for pants.

To connect with Inessa:

For book coaching and editing, visit:
www.inessasage.com

To read Inessa's books, visit: www.ansage.ca

Connect on Social Media:

Instagram:
https://www.instagram.com/a.n.sage

Facebook:
https://www.facebook.com/ansagewrites

or join her author Facebook group: https://www.facebook.com/groups/945090619339423

YouTube:
https://www.youtube.com/@ANSageWrites

TikTok:
https://www.tiktok.com/@ansagewrites